A MINGLED YARN

by the same author

JACKSON'S YEAR
MINISTRY OF SONG
EARLY TOURS IN DEVON AND CORNWALL

A MINGLED YARN

Alan Gibson

'The web of our life is of a mingled yarn, good
and ill together: our virtues would be proud
if our faults whipped them not; and our crimes
would despair if they were not cherished by
our own virtues.'

ALL'S WELL THAT ENDS WELL
ACT IV, SCENE III

COLLINS
St James's Place, London
1976

William Collins Sons & Co Ltd
London · Glasgow · Sydney · Auckland
Toronto · Johannesburg

First published 1976

ISBN 0 00 216115 X

Set in Monotype Perpetua
Made and Printed in Great Britain by
William Collins Sons & Co Ltd Glasgow

to ROSEMARY

Sero te amavi, pulchritudo tam antiqua
et tam nova, sero te amavi

Contents

	Foreword	9
1	Ilkley	11
2	Leyton	25
3	Jordan	35
4	Munich	48
5	Oxford	57
6	Devon	77
7	Plymouth	93
8	Sparkwell	103
9	Babel	120
10	Tin Pan Alley	129
11	Lord's and Twickenham	148
12	Cornwall	167
13	Moorhaven	190
14	Bristol	207
15	Beulah	216

Foreword

I think it was George Orwell who said, 'Autobiography is only to be trusted when it is disgraceful,' on which basis at least some passages in this book are trustworthy. Certainly it was A. L. Rowse who said, 'I do not know that an autobiography requires an apology. Autobiographies to my mind make interesting reading.' This was in the introduction to *A Cornish Childhood*, a compelling book, which sees Nonconformity in a different light from mine.

I agree with both these statements. I have not been entirely truthful about myself – who can be? It is a scattered sort of book about a scattered sort of life. Perhaps it illustrates some of the advantages and disadvantages of an upbringing in English religious Dissent. A good book, like a good sermon, often tells you more than its author intends, and I hope, or possibly fear, that it may be so with this one.

Alan Gibson

Clifton, Bristol, 1975

1 Ilkley

I was born at Sheffield in 1923. My father was a poorly paid Baptist minister in Attercliffe, a down-town district. Yet that, for him, was a step upward. He had been born in 1890, and had started working in the mine at Spennymoor, county Durham, in 1902. His formal education was therefore negligible, though he always remembered the black strap at school. He managed to educate himself sufficiently to win a place at Spurgeon's College in order to train for the Baptist ministry. In the first world war, when all the gentlemen officers had been killed off, and the net had to be cast wider, he obtained a commission in the Durham Light Infantry, and did well. He was gassed in the German advance in the spring of 1918, which affected his eyes and indeed his general health. He was a good and successful minister, much loved, and – although I know this is the kind of thing people tend to say of their fathers, I have no doubt of it – a saint: not as a Catholic would use the word, but as Milton and Isaac Watts did.

My mother was born of a respectable family in South Shields, the daughter of a sailing-ship master who later, reluctantly, turned to steam; and also, spasmodically, to strong drink. Mother was a Methodist, as were all her family, and she continued to hold rigid views on such subjects as Sabbatarianism and total abstinence for the rest of her life. She married my father in 1922, and I am their only son. A daughter was born some years after me, but lived for only nine months.

Both my father and mother were members of large families

– thirteen on father's side, eight on mother's, if I remember rightly. Many of them survived and had families in their turn. Thus I have always had an ample supply of aunts, uncles and cousins, but since most of them stayed in the north, and we soon left for the south, my contacts with them have been intermittent.

In 1967 I spoke at a dinner in Sheffield, in the Cutlers' Hall, held by the Sheffield Cricket Lovers' Association for the Indian touring team. This would have pleased father. Attercliffe Church was then a derelict ruin waiting for the demolition men, not very far away. I was glad to be introduced as a local lad, but Sheffield has not had much influence in my life. Certainly it gave me an unchallengeable Yorkshire qualification at cricket, but that turned out to be a purely theoretical advantage. Before I was two we moved to Ilkley, which I thought then, and expect is still, a good place to live.

The first clear recollection I have is of blackberrying with my mother on the banks of the river Wharfe, keeping my own share in a small crumpled bag which had previously contained sweets, and watching the white paper slowly turn purple with the juice. I got to know that beautiful stretch of Wharfedale well. The great treat was an outing to Bolton Abbey, and a picnic by the stepping stones, and then in the afternoon a ride in pony and trap, up river, to the Strid. Here the Wharfe is compressed into a narrow rock-bound channel, foaming tumultuously through a gap no wider than a tall man's stride. But it was a risky stride, since the rocks on both sides are slippery. The river there, I was told, was fifty-three feet deep – I have no idea whether this is so, but that was certainly what I was told, and the figure is etched on my mind. Father had striden across once, but not when I was there, and I trembled at the thought of what might have happened to him. For I was also told that the gap between the rocks widened downwards in the shape of an inverted 'V', so that if you fell in you could never hope to be rescued. This is the place of which Wordsworth wrote in 'Bolton Priory'. For a long way below the Strid, before it gradually broadened again to its placid and cheerful self, the Wharfe stayed dark, sullen, foam-splotched, ominous. The black depths were worse than the white turbulence, and I dreamed of them at nights.

We lived very close to the Wharfe at Ilkley, in Middleton Road, leading to the Old Bridge. Since the New Bridge had been built, further east, the Old Bridge had been barred to motor traffic. It was narrow and humped, though solid-looking. My father constantly had occasion to traverse the Old Bridge on his pastoral visiting. He owned a motor-scooter, an object of some mirth in those days, and he had an informal arrangement with the police, whereby he would hop off his scooter, run it over the Old Bridge, keeping the engine going (it took hard work on the handle to restart it) and hop on again, on the other side. One day a new and zealous constable, who did not know of this arrangement, heard the continuous buzz of the engine and promptly booked father. It was quite a *cause celebre* in Ilkley, and I was very alarmed lest he should go to prison, but he was triumphantly acquitted. Another time I was playing by the Old Bridge when a runaway horse came tearing down the hill towards it, dragging a shambles of a milk cart, and missed me by a few inches. This must have been the nearest I have been to death, except once. It did not, apparently, alarm me much at the time, although it nearly petrified several onlookers, including my poor mother, who dared not call to me as she was on the other side of the road, with the horse's path in between.

On either side of Ilkley and of the Wharfe lay the moors: Ilkley Moor to the south, Middleton Moor to the north. Incidentally, I do not remember hearing that stupid song about Ilkley Moor in my years there; I doubt if Ilkley people sang it much. I knew the tune, certainly, but that was because it was set in the hymn-book to the words of Doddridge,

> Grace! 'Tis a charming sound,
> Harmonious to the ear,
> Heaven with the echo shall resound
> And all the earth shall hear!

Very well it went, too. Old Tom Clark, the cobbler who became leader of psalmody in the Wesleyan church, set the tune to the words early in the nineteenth century. He called it 'Cranbrook', as a Kentish man should, and I doubt if it originated anywhere near Ilkley at all.

Ilkley Moor, though friendly enough in its foothills, was a stern barrier high on the skyline, cutting off the setting sun and making early twilight in winter. On its edge was the paddling pool, in which I regularly sat down. A little further up was the Tarn, where it was a much more serious matter to fall in. I nevertheless did so, once, and was much more perturbed than I had been by the runaway horse. In fact I recall clearly feeling how sad it was that such a promising life should be wasted, in the few seconds before father hauled me out. There was the White Wells, a beacon half way to the top, which the eye picked up at once on the dullest day. Above the White Wells was the mystery of wilderness. Up there was the Rocky Valley. The Rocky Valley: it was the first phrase that ever gave me the sense of words as poetry. Every time I go back to Ilkley I plan to visit the Rocky Valley, but I never have done. I am afraid lest it prove less rocky, less deep, less romantic than it is pictured by the memories of childhood. The Cow and Calf rocks, which tip the moor's eastern end, were rather different. The Cow could be approached without difficulty – you could even get a bus most of the way – and it was splendid to sit on the rock's flat top, a safe distance from the edge, and survey the dale below.

Middleton Moor was gentler. That was the place for the blackberries in the autumn, and the bluebells in the spring. There must have been primroses too, but it is the bluebells I remember, the bluebells that were the glory of Middleton woods. Only once have I seen greater masses of them, and that was at Start Point, in Devon. But on the Start the bluebells are inviolate on the steep escarpment, and in Middleton woods they were easily gathered by everyone, yet still never seemed to grow less.

They were happy years in Ilkley. I was, I think, an obstreperous child, but I loved my parents, and they loved me and each other. Despite the strictness of their moral code, which was less strange in the 1920s than it would be today, they were anything but stern disciplinarians. I had a lot of fun, and was never severely punished when I was naughty. Sundays, to be sure, were rather a bore, but I liked most of the chapel people and had no objection to Sunday School. I knew nothing of the horrors which, for instance, Edmund Gosse described in *Father and Son*. There was no stamping of sinful and illicit Christmas puddings into the rubbish heap. I was in my mid teens before I began seriously to question my parents' views about anything. Of course, beer was wrong, and so were shops that opened on Sundays – though the latter reminds me of a curious incident. There was in Ilkley a specially good ice-cream shop run by Mrs Stone (ice-cream in shops was permissible: ice-cream from itinerant vendors was still frowned upon). Mrs Stone, unfortunately, kept her shop open on Sundays. Mother and I would go to Mrs Stone's for an ice-cream, but father, because of his position, could not. So there we were at Mrs Stone's while father took his ice-cream in another shop, a couple of doors away, where the product was inferior but the Sabbath was observed. Just why this distinction between us was made I cannot recall or understand. Perhaps it was simply that I expressed my preference for Mrs Stone's ice-cream very strongly, and they were reluctant to disappoint me.

I went to school at the age of four. 'Grove School, Ilkley' was a school 'for girls and little boys'. The Grove was the promenade of Ilkley, and the name had an air about it, although the building was in a side-street from the Grove. The little boys had bright green and yellow caps made up in alternate triangles, and I was extremely proud of mine. I would take it off smartly to members of the congregation, and beamingly introduce myself with a little bob: 'Alan Gibson – Schoolboy!' (How insufferable. I do not myself remember this, but mother always insisted it was true.)

Miss Wilkinson ran the school, and in my second year there she became, to our interest, Mrs Rhodes. I have no idea what her qualifications were as a teacher, but she was a kind person, and I owe to her my first interest in history, a subject in which she was obviously interested herself, and about which she spoke effectively. The first history essay – 'composition' was the word used – I can remember writing was about the descent of the fireships on the Armada. I tried to illustrate it, as requested, but I have never been able to draw. But I got good marks for 'writing'. I have always found pleasure in putting words together, at least when I can make them fit. Few delights in life compare with the rare and difficult achievement of writing a sound piece of English prose. This I began to learn from Mrs Rhodes; for me it was the most important thing to be learnt.

Father had at Ilkley a good and dutiful congregation. It was not so large as it had been at Sheffield, but much wealthier. It would be wrong to suggest it was a snobbish congregation, but there was a substantial percentage of wool merchants and rentiers. Canny Yorkshire folk, they did not believe in over-paying their minister, but they would be generous with gifts to him, and to his family. At Christmas not a stocking but a pillow-case was needed for my presents. How vividly I remember the day my father was presented with that marvel of modern science, that symbol of the high-powered business life, a typewriter! It was a Remington portable, and it lasted father, and after him me, a total of twenty-five years. (It was the same type of machine that Frank Richards used for his millions of words, and oddly enough father shared Frank Richards's *penchant* for purple ribbons.)

The typewriter was a gift from the Miss Newboults. There were four Miss Newboults, living together in a big house called 'Fairfield', just over the Old Bridge. Their names, in order of seniority, were Miss Ada, Miss Mary, Miss Minnie and Miss Florrie. Miss Ada was friendly but remote. Miss Mary was kind, very short-sighted: I could usually get round Miss Mary. Miss Minnie was upright, business-like, and could be stern: she once, when we were paying a return visit to Ilkley and staying with the Newboults, took away from me a newspaper in which I was reading of the last day in a dramatic murder trial. 'There are some things,' said Miss Minnie, 'which Little Boys *should not read*.' This was not a hard penance, however, since I had been puzzling over what 'acquitted' meant, and everything depended on that. It was years before I found this out. I thought 'acquittal' was probably some ferocious form of punishment.

It was the trial of Mrs Barney, when, in the face of formidable prosecution evidence, Sir Patrick Hastings conducted what is considered by many lawyers to be the greatest defence of his career.

Miss Florrie was the youngest Newboult, plump and jolly,

and I adored her. In all my life I have loved few people so much. How old was she, I wonder? All the Miss Newboults seemed very old to me, but Miss Florrie cannot, when I first knew her, have been much over forty. All the same, that was quite an age to play cricket with a small and often tiresome child, for hours on end, and then go indoors and play halma or draughts or patience (cards were permitted) for hours more. Yet this she constantly did. I am sure Miss Florrie had a happy and useful life, although it ended too soon (she was the first of the four sisters to die). It seems an impertinence to wish she had married and had a family, and possibly she herself would have been shocked at the idea; but she had a wonderful knack of getting on with children.

The Miss Newboults, and the others of their generation in Ilkley Baptist Church in the 1920s, were the last of the Victorian Dissenters. This is a category which in my lifetime has come in for heavy abuse. I have grown away from some (though not all) of their beliefs and traditions. Yet there is one point I would stress about them, which is not always remembered: they were *happy* people. 'Jolly' would be a better word, except that nowadays it carries unfortunate overtones. There was always a lot of laughter among chapel people. Mr Eastwood, who was something important in a bank, and the church treasurer, had a broad smile which seemed larger than all the rest of him, like the Cheshire cat. Mr Haley, who had a very posh house on the Ben Rhydding road (Ilkley's Mayfair), and a lavish car, with chauffeur, in which he would often take us all for a day's outing – Mr Haley, who was driven into his big office in Bradford every day, who was (I was given to understand) in regular consultation with the government about the affairs of the wool trade, was a nutcracker of a man when he was not in church. He was the type of Yorkshireman who can be a good talker but not a bore, telling stories not because he was anxious to show off but because the good humour brimmed out of him. He also had a place in his life for quietness and reverence. Mr Haley was regarded with suspicion by the more proletarian members of the congregation because he was a 'oncer' (Sunday mornings only: in the evenings he had dinner, another suspicious circumstance, because dinner-time was normally in the middle of the day). Mr Haley gave father a gold pen, which was considered a little ostentatious, though not by father, who had never had a fountain pen of any kind before.

Nobody who has lived with the Dissenters, if his experience even approximates to mine, could think of them as a harsh or bitter people. Nor, I think, has this ever been the case. The idea of the Puritans as gloomy killjoys does not stand up to examination. The first section of the eighth chapter of J. R. Green's *Short History of the English People* describes the Puritans of the seventeenth century much as I have known the Puritans of the twentieth. Milton's youth, says Green, 'shews us how much of the gaiety, the poetic ease, the intellectual culture of the Renascence lingered in a Puritan home.' It lingered a long time. My home and my background – throughout my father's ministry and in widely varying places – were not uncultured and were always gay.

Yet the theology they accepted was far from gay. My father was the kind of person whom people describe as a man of 'gentle piety'. He was gentle and he was pious, but that is only a part of the picture. He believed in hell, though as he once said 'we don't know whether there's anyone in it or not'. He believed in judgement. He believed that sin should be condemned. He would not accept a woman into his church who was an adulteress (unless, to be sure, she repented and put it behind her). He believed in the sin against the Holy Ghost: that is, the sin against the light. He believed that the Bible was

God's Word, with the usual reservations about the early historical parts of the Old Testament. He believed that the Church of Rome was a gross distortion of the faith once committed to the saints.

Now these things may be true, indeed I believe some of them are. But to say such things of a man does not conjure up a picture of a gay man. Yet that too he was. This was the negative side of his faith. The positive side was a love for his Master which really made the gospel, in his mouth, good news, something to be gay about. Nor was this in any way the kind of jolly-them-along-all-boys-and-girls-together attitude which a lot of parsons affected then and still do, and which makes for such wincing moments. It was a natural, unforced happiness which infected all those around him; it was Protestant Dissent at its best.

All the same, father had considerable toughness, inherited from one side of his family. About eighty years ago there was a well-known County Durham character, always to be seen at the Miners' Gala, called Cheap Jack. His real name was John Boyle, and he was my great-grandfather. Cheap Jack was a poet, and used to travel the county selling his verses, and anything else he could. I have never found any examples of his poetry, though I have often enquired. He was also a temperance lecturer, which was probably at that time a more lucrative undertaking. Every year at the gala he would speak upon the folly of drinking, and his audiences enjoyed his eloquence, even if they did not always follow his precepts. He was an enthusiastic politician, and family tradition has it that he would have been the Liberal candidate for Sunderland, and probably elected to the Commons, except that he lacked a formal education, and his poetic abilities were not held to be sufficient compensation.

In the year 1896 his daughter – my grandmother – left

Spennymoor by an early train to join her husband in Sunderland. She was twenty-nine years old, and had six children with her, the oldest eight years old, the youngest six months. Her husband was supposed to have found a job and a dwelling in Sunderland, but when she got there she found he had neither, and was off on a booze. These little weaknesses of his would last for several days at a time; he must have found the responsibility of being son-in-law to Cheap Jack rather severe.

The only thing for grandmother to do was to return to her parents' home at Spennymoor; but she had no money for the fares, beyond Durham. However, it was Gala day – 'Big Meeting Day' – at Durham, and she knew her father would be about somewhere, so she set out to find him. The crowds were large, she was hampered by the six small children, and she soon realized she did not have much chance of success.

When she was on the point of despair – and it took something to make my grandmother despair – a horse and cart passed by, carrying a load of boxes of bottled lemonade. She called out to the carter: 'Mister! Will ye let me have that loored o' lemonayud?' She explained that her husband had got lost on the way (which was more or less true), and her stall had not turned up either (an invention on the spur of the moment), but she could make a stall out of the boxes, and start business; and then, if the carter came back with another load, she could pay him for the first.

He must have been a kind man, that carter. He agreed. Up went the stall of boxes: lemonade tuppence a bottle, drunk straight from the bottles with their glass marbles for stoppers. As soon as a few shillings had been taken, grandmother sent Jessie, the eight-year-old, to the shops: to buy a washing-up bowl, six glasses, two cloths, and a basket for the baby. When the carter returned with his second load, he was paid for the first, and asked to bring another. Those children who were old enough, including my father, who was six, did what they could to help. All day long the stall kept going. In the evening grandmother packed up, and went to an inn nearby, where the landlord took her shillings and sixpences and pennies, and gave her in return over twenty pounds, mostly in golden sovereigns. Grandmother, in telling the story, always relished the bit about the sovereigns.

All of them stayed the night at the inn, and next day they had another unprecedented luxury, returning to Spennymoor by horse and trap; and still when they got there, a substantial balance was in hand. Mrs Gibson's Lemonade Stall, later raised to the dignity of Mrs Gibson's Refreshment Tent, was to be found at the Gala every year until 1914, giving its annual boost to the family fortunes. I have a photograph of it, my father as chief attendant in a white apron. After the first war, it ceased to be a family concern, but the name survived for a while, and for all I know it still does.

When unemployment struck the Durham miners so severely in the twenties, upon grandmother's initiative most of the family moved to Blackpool, where she ran a boarding-house, and in time several of her daughters ran their own. Grandmother packed in the guests (she denied she let late arrivals sleep in the bath, but I am not sure). 'FOUR KNIFE AND FORK MEALS A DAY!' she had in her window. I doubt if she ever made much money, because of grandfather's genial habit of drinking the profits, but she kept the family going. I was slightly alarmed by grandmother, vast and black and beaded. She was chairman of the Blackpool Women's Liberals at one point, and said to be the only person who could keep Edgar Wallace in order when he was the candidate there.

I was not, however, to see very much of her, or of the rest of the family in the north, because when I was seven years old father had a call to Vicarage Road Baptist Church, Leyton, in

London. Perhaps I should explain that in the Baptist ministry there is no superior authority which switches ministers round from church to church, though there is an advisory service to help in cases of difficulty. Ministers are elected by the churches. It was because of this emphasis on the importance of election that the rise of Dissent, in both England and America, went hand in hand with the development of parliamentary institutions. If a minister feels led, in prayer (or possibly because of an awkward congregation), he can today let his name go forward to the area superintendent, who circulates it in the churches which are themselves without ministers or looking for a change. Then follows the frequently harrowing business of 'preaching with a view': taking the Sunday services at the churches which have expressed interest. Father had moved to Ilkley from Sheffield, chiefly because of a breakdown in his health. Five years of the Ilkley air had set him up again, at least for the time being. Ilkley was too comfortable a number, as we would say now, for a young minister who was also mildly ambitious. He decided to move. Leyton was the first, and on that occasion the only place at which he preached with a view. They asked him to come, at a salary of £250, which was, I think, £25 more than he was getting at Ilkley. He also had a disability pension, and lived in the Manse rent-free (though in all my father's ministry we only lived in one comfortable Manse). We were fairly well off by the standards of Baptist ministers, still more by the standards of Leyton at that time.

I knew there was something in the air. One afternoon the Miss Newboults called, all in their Sunday clothes although it was a weekday, all looking very solemn and sad, and went with father and mother into the front room (normally only used at Sunday tea-time). They had come to make a last appeal to father not to go. He said later that had they come in the morning he would never have gone, but that he had posted the letter of acceptance at lunchtime. I am not quite sure about that. At the time he believed he had a 'true call'. Many years afterwards he also believed it had been a true call. But in the interim he came to doubt it, and bitterly to regret leaving Ilkley. For there was a period of much trouble in store for him and my mother, and even – though I was too young to be miserable for long – for me. After a last glorious Christmas at Ilkley, when even a pillow-case was not enough and a bolster-case had to be used to hold my presents, we moved to Leyton in the first weeks of 1930. The first thing I remember noticing was how dirty the station was. The second was that there were no fields. The third, more appealing, was how noisy the trams were. The fourth, which had I known it already contained the seeds of redemption, was that the house overlooked the Essex county cricket ground.

2 Leyton

If you live in a place long enough you are bound to become attached to it. I once knew an ex-prisoner who would occasionally become sentimental about the 'dear old Scrubs'. For myself I have usually lived in pleasant places. Leyton was the least pleasant, but there were good times, and I grew fond of it.

Not for some while, however. For quite a long time, on going to bed, or on waking in the middle of the night, I would try to persuade myself that Leyton was just a nasty dream, and that in the morning I would be back in my little room at Ilkley, with the line of the moors high on the horizon. Leyton in 1930 was rapidly losing its individuality, and becoming just an extension of the East End.

School, too, took some getting used to. I went to Farmer Road, the big elementary school at the end of the street where we lived. Big? After Grove School, Ilkley, 'Farmer' was vast beyond belief. There were more boys and girls in my class in the infants' department than in Mrs Rhodes's entire command. Furthermore, I could not understand much of what they said – a difficulty they shared in reverse. For they were all Cockneys, and I had acquired a fairly broad Yorkshire accent. One of my schoolmates went home to his mother at lunchtime on my first day and announced, 'We've got a Frenchman in our class.'

Incidentally, anyone who wants to speak what is called 'standard English' (though I have never thought it mattered much) would do well to live in different parts of the country in childhood and youth. One accent seems to cancel another out, but without depriving speech of colour and character, as 'elocutionary' English does.

The poverty in Leyton was not extreme, compared with many other places in those days, but bad enough, and shocking to me after Ilkley. The commonest excuse for playing truant was 'no boots'. It often *was* only an excuse, but likely enough to be true in some cases to make the masters accept it.

'Help the Boot Fund' was the school slogan. Apart from the boots, many of the boys were often ill, the mildest of germs ravaging their under-nourished bodies. At the age of nine I moved from the infants' department to the junior school, and 'The Scholarship' began to loom on the horizon. This was much the same as the eleven-plus, though we did not know that term then, and it carried the same dread consequences: ordeal by bicycle, and all the rest of it. Fortunately I always enjoyed examinations, and in consequence did better in them than I deserved. Fortunately, too, for two years I had the advantage of being taught by Arthur Bird, one of the best schoolmasters I ever met. This judgement is not nostalgic. I met him many years later in Cornwall, where he had retired, and he was every bit as wise and kind as I had always believed him to be.

I have a picture of Arthur Bird's Class One: the *élite* of the junior school, the class from which might possibly emerge someone capable of passing the scholarship. Farmer Road had got two boys into the grammar school in two years, which was considered good going for such a school. When Arthur Bird took us through we got nine, which was hardly believable, including the top boy at Leyton Grammar School, and the top boy at Sir George Monoux Grammar School, Walthamstow (that was I: father had put me down for this neighbouring school because, I suspect, he thought there was a certain mystique about the title, pronounced Monux). The top boy at Leyton Grammar School was John Durnford Cook. He was also top in the whole of Essex, I coming a miserable third.

I am surprised I have heard no more of Jack Cook.

These results were as big a triumph, given the conditions, as most schoolmasters could hope to have. There are thirty-nine boys in my picture of Class One. The full strength of the class, if it was ever mustered, must have been nearer fifty than forty. I edited a class magazine, which I typed out each week-end on the Remington portable. Constantly I got the ribbon tangled, constantly father patiently untangled it. He did not, however, share in the writing of the paper. *The Farmer Weekly* was my own; my first attempt at journalism. It began, indeed, while we were still 'Class Four', as the following excerpt testifies. I still have the original, which is too tattered to reproduce. But, as nearly as I can, I copy out the typing.

```
                THE FARMER WEEKLY.       Page One.
                      Edited by N.A.S.Gibson (Class Four, Junior
        School);
                     Masters-Mr.Thompson, Mr.Davies, Mr.Downing, Mr.Bird,
Mr.Dreghorn. Mr.Appleby. Mr.Fuller.
                      Mistresses Miss Walker & Mrs ————————.
Headmaster-Mr.Patternoster.
                      Note-This Magazine Apply's to Junior School only.

                      LATEST SPORTS.
                        Football.
                27th Sept., Results.
                        Green 1.  Yellow 0;
                        Blue 1.  Red 0;
                        Blue 0. Green 0;


                                    OUR SPORTS NOTES. By Left-half.
The twenty-sevenths matches were very successful. For the Green v
Yellow match a draw was the fairest result, but an error by T.Davis,
who headed through his own goal off Defries' corner, in the Final
minute, spoilt Yellow's chances. Apart from this Davis played a
thoroughly soubd game.
Blue deserved to beat Red, although Pate shewed up well in goal for
the losers. Watts played a fine game at centre-forward. In the Final
game a terrific fight ensued, Slee played well in goal for Blue,
Watts was again brilliant. Once Watts was nearly through, but he was
brought to a full stop by Eagle. It will be interesting to note that
on Friday, Class Four go to Ive Farm with Mr.Dreghorn, to play Football.
Weall hope it will be a fine day.

                              NEXT FRIDAY'S CONCERT. By Listener.
The winning colour last week was Yellow, therefore the Yellowites
give a concert on Friday. Cook (Class Four) will give a Yo-Yo .
exhibition, and the Editor is hoping to do some conjuring tricks.
The concert should be successful. The Editor has not yet ascertained
whether Verrill is doing the conjuring trick he said he could do.
```

A touch of heavy sarcasm here by the arts critic, and clearly no lack of readiness to publicize the exploits of N. A. S. Gibson, who was always referred to in his columns as 'The Editor'. In a later edition, I see that 'The Editor scored 5 goals.' Can this be true? I would scarcely have dared to publish it if it were not, but the mind retains no memory of such a feat.

Later, *The Farmer Weekly* became much more sophisticated. There was a powerful series of articles (by The Editor) entitled 'A Holiday in Lakeland!' The first one was entitled, 'Lakeside, Windermere.' The first sentence ran:

The glory of the Scene almost took your Breath away! There was a series of 'Personal Pars' (the style was copied from the local football programme), which included this comment on Mr Bird:

Ought to have got a Headmastership by Now.

And this devastating summary of an unfortunate boy called Binks:

Very insignificant in the class.

Any surplus space was always filled in with a hand-written advertisement, in large capitals: 'HELP THE BOOT FUND!!'

The mention of Ive Farm brings back memories (so does the mention of Mr Dreghorn, a cheerful young man who always wore a red tie and was popularly believed to be in direct touch by wireless with Moscow). Farmer Road had, of course, no playing fields. In recreation periods – themselves a daring innovation – we played soccer with a tennis ball on stone playgrounds. (Incidentally, the post-war rise of rugby in schools, a better game for growing boys to play, has more to do with the decline of stone playgrounds than with snobbery, as is sometimes suggested.) There was much excitement when the Leyton Education Committee acquired Ive Farm, a real grass field. It was shared by about a dozen schools, and it was, or seemed, miles away from ours: but the long trudge there and back, though it took up nearly half the double-period allotted to recreation, was well worth it for the joy of playing on a proper ground. Not Lord's, not Wembley, not even Twickenham will ever have quite the same magic ring for me as Ive Farm.

Today, Farmer Road still stands, as ugly as ever in its heavy red brick, but in other ways transformed. It is the George Mitchell County Secondary School (by the time you read this, it may be something else, for better or worse). George Mitchell was a Farmer Road pupil who won the VC in Italy in the second world war. A year or two ago I revisited the school, and I quote some information from the headmaster's annual report. Sixty-one passes were obtained in GCE. Eight boys went on to do sixth form work at the high school. There were facilities for woodwork, metalwork, technical drawing (commonplace now, no doubt, but inconceivable in 1933). The school ran twenty teams: four soccer, four rugby, four cricket, three basketball, three cross-country, two swimming. The swimming team actually won the Borough Gala by beating High (Grammar) School by what the Head called 'a glorious all-sufficient one point'. I was deeply moved by this information. Think of it, my old fellow-Farmerians, Jack Cook and Howard ('Podgy') Pate and Raymond Slee and the rest of you, if ever this meets your eye! To beat the infinitely remote and superior High School at swimming! In those days hardly any of us could even swim, for few of us had the chance; and most of us only saw the sea at Sunday School outings.

Sunday School outings is a theme to stir the memory. Only a few years ago, when I was introducing a record request programme, I received a letter from some children, with the footnote (it was an early morning programme) 'Please play it before 8.30, because then we are leaving for the Sunday School outing.' I did not know that Sunday School outings still existed. I am certain that they can only be pale shadows of those glorious occasions of my childhood.

Sunday School outings, for me, mean Westcliff in the early thirties. I stress that it was Westcliff, not Southend. Westcliff carried a certain social cachet. That mile up the estuary made all the difference. Only the better Sunday Schools went to Westcliff. It was one of the ways in which Vicarage Road Baptist demonstrated that Leyton was still a cut above Hackney.

Qualification for the outing was a tense business. The regulations were fairly generous – if I remember, thirty-five attendances a year was the requirement – but there were always those who had neglected their spiritual duties in the autumn, when Westcliff was far away, and were struggling to catch up. Then there were those who had only recently joined. It was possible, if you found three schools whose outings were a month apart, to join all three in succession, and go on three outings. The chief safeguard against this sort of skullduggery lay in the faithful, who were swift to question any newcomer's background, and report to authority if he seemed likely to gain an uncovenanted benefit. But in the end I think nearly everyone who wanted to go on our outing went, since my father, the final court of appeal, found it difficult to refuse a child anything. Each year Tommy Watts would turn up for Sunday School just three weeks before the outing; each year father would extract a solemn promise from him that he would be regular in his devotions in future; and each year Tommy would be off – we suspected, O horror! to the Roman Catholics – immediately the outing was over. He is now probably a pillar of the ecumenical movement.

When I say my father could refuse a child nothing, I must make certain exceptions concerning myself. My own qualifications for the outing were never in doubt, since I was despatched to Sunday School with ruthless regularity. One Sunday afternoon I announced, experimentally, that I didn't feel like going: the only response was a kindly, rather puzzled smile, and of course I went just the same. Once, for some grievous sin the nature of which I strangely cannot remember, I was threatened with exclusion from the outing. I was forgiven in the end, but I remember how alarming a threat it seemed – surprisingly so, since after all I was a child who had a proper holiday (sometimes in Lakeland!) every year, a holiday lasting for two or even three weeks.

The outings themselves come back in a blurred kaleidoscope rather than an ordered sequence of memory. There was the seething platform at Leyton LMS station, that grubby station perched high above the arches – a constant miracle it was that nobody fell off either forwards on to the line or backwards on to the street below. Half a dozen special excursion trains would go through before ours arrived, all of them crammed to bursting with children. Then, the great moment: a train with empty compartments and labels on the windows:

VIC RD BAP

The sea was always out when we arrived at Westcliff, but there was the diversion of watching those who, for supposed medicinal reasons, would walk out and roll themselves in the estuary mud. Half the Sunday School would immediately try to do the same, with teachers dashing in all directions to restrain them. By the afternoon the water had come in, and there was bathing, even swimming for a few. Those risky devices known as 'water wings' were in great demand, and the teachers who could swim were constantly on duty, rescuing children who had come adrift from their water wings while out of their depth. No one was ever drowned, but there were some near things.

There were shrimps, beautiful orange-pink shrimps, a penny a packet, the seaside equivalent of a pennorth o' chips. There was also, of course, the fascination of young members of the opposite sex getting dressed and undressed on the beaches. It was at Westcliff that I discovered the essential fact about the female anatomy. All those confusing lessons about bees and catkins had not helped at all, though I am sure they were less unpleasant than the drab detail of a BBC sex-instruction film. Once you realized how a girl was made the thing became obvious. I am not suggesting there was any youthful promiscuity on these occasions. I never encountered any. We were of an age to be interested rather than stirred.

Then there was the panic when the train home was due, and five children still missing, teachers once again despatched in all directions (I marvel, looking back, at their kindness – giving up one of their few precious days' holiday for such a back-breaking chore). One year Tommy Watts never turned up for the train at all, and we left without him. For weeks afterwards he entertained us with tales of his wild night at Southend, and I expect he is still dining out with his fellow-bishops on the story; but as a matter of fact all that happened was that he caught the next train, unhurried and also unharried because he had frequently been a member of *that* Sunday School too, and at that time of evening no one was in a mood to split doctrinal hairs.

I do not remember it raining on any of these occasions. As the minister's son I went on a variety of church outings, sometimes not very willingly, but because I could hardly be left alone at home. Rain bedevilled the trips of the PMA ('Pleasant Monday Afternoons' – the women's meeting), the choir, and the Bible Class. The Crusaders, the Boys' Brigade, the Church Fellowship and the Band of Hope never set forth without the heavens opening. But not once do I recall a drop of rain falling on the Sunday School. Each year we would come back scorched and peeling. At the time I confidently attributed this to the power of prayer. I am not sure that I was altogether wrong.

By the time I was about ten I was expected to go to church twice on Sundays, as well as afternoon Sunday School (morning Sunday School, before church, I was mercifully excused). I still did not much enjoy Sundays, and to this day I relish the thought, when I wake up on Sunday morning, that I do not need to go to church unless I wish to go. But this was not a major unhappiness, and I found Leyton improved on acquaintance.

The cricket ground was the godsend. From the top balcony we could see a big chunk of the field, and the scoreboard; and on Saturdays it was only sixpence to go in. Essex played nearly all their home matches there. Thus began one of the most enriching experiences of my life; but I have written of early cricketing days elsewhere.

In the winter I would go to see Leyton (Athenian League) play football, since I was thought to be too small to hazard the crowds at Highbury or White Hart Lane (once or twice I was taken to Upton Park, the West Ham ground, when father could afford two stand seats). It was no hardship to watch Leyton, since they were an excellent amateur club, who twice in those years reached the Amateur Cup final. What disturbed me was that their best players kept leaving to go to neighbouring clubs, for reasons I can understand better now than then. Leyton suffered a severe blow when their ground was taken over (by some rather sharp practice, or so we believed) by Clapton Orient, who later had the nerve to pinch Leyton's name as well. I still feel an atavistic satisfaction if I hear that Orient (for they have abandoned the 'Leyton' as coolly as they commandeered it) have had a good beating. Leyton fell on bad times after the war, but a few years ago turned up as Athenian League champions, and I was surprised how pleased I was. Then, according to a press report, the manager and half the team decamped to Dagenham, or some such place, and Leyton dropped two divisions in two seasons. Poor Leyton. That was the kind of thing that always happened to them.

It was much more serious when Essex left Leyton, left it altogether for many years, though they now go back to that same ground for one week a year. Essex had been my favourites, after Yorkshire of course, but I was so cross with them that they too became for years objurgated. It was only in middle age, after coming to know Trevor Bailey, that I could bring myself once more to think kindly of Essex cricket.

It was in 1934 that Essex left, the same year as I progressed from Farmer Road to Monoux. I had been too preoccupied with the scholarship, to say nothing of *The Farmer Weekly*, to worry much about my soul at this time. But the heavy diet of worship was bound to have its effect, and soon I began to worry about it very much indeed.

3 Jordan

There is often confusion, even among Christians, as to what Baptists believe. They have only slender connections with the Anabaptists of the sixteenth and seventeenth centuries, who held extreme political views, and were among the wildest (though also the most interesting) of the sectaries. The Baptist Union of Great Britain and Northern Ireland is an orthodox Protestant body, holding the 'independent' view of the nature of church government, and usually taking a strong line on vice. Only fifteen years ago, or thereabouts, the annual assembly called upon all Baptists to become total abstainers, but the resolution was a dead letter. The local church, not the assembly, is the final authority, and any church may admit to membership anyone whom it sees fit.

Baptists take their name from the views they hold on the sacrament of baptism, though it is not only Baptists who hold these views. Baptism is of believers. The important thing about it is not, as many imagine, the method – it is usually by immersion, but that is in no way essential – but that the person being baptized must have *chosen* to be. It is a public declaration of his faith, which nobody else may make for him. It usually takes place at about the age of an Anglican confirmation, but sacramentally the two are distinct. Infants are not baptized: they are dedicated to the Church by their parents. Hence – often a source of slight disappointment to themselves, as well as to friends and relations – Baptist children have no godparents. Oddly enough, the rubric of the Anglican service prescribes immersion as the proper form of baptism, unless the child is certified to be weak. H. B.

Swete, when a curate, was accused of being a Baptist for observing it.

But though baptism by immersion is not essential, it does provide a very striking illustration of what is intended by the act.

'When we descended into the baptismal water, that meant that we died with Christ – to sin. When the water closed over our heads, that meant that we lay buried with Him, in proof that our death to sin, like His death, was real. But this carries with it the third step in the process. As Christ was raised from the dead by a majestic exercise of Divine power, so we also must from henceforth conduct ourselves as men in whom has been implanted a new principle of life.'[1]

The public ceremony of baptism can be very beautiful. It can also be ludicrous. Some years ago I broadcast a commentary on a televised baptismal service from Emmanuel Baptist Church, Falmouth (which had been one of my father's churches). Emmanuel is a handsome church with a permanently open baptistery, well designed for its purpose. The candidate steps into the well of the baptistery from the church, and steps straight out into the dressing-rooms. On that occasion everything passed off admirably, but they were tense moments. Kenneth Savidge, the producer, an Anglican, said to me afterwards: 'You Baptists do tread on some very thin ice,' and his meaning was clear despite a certain inexactitude of metaphor. In many older churches the baptistery is buried beneath the floorboards, and is usually ugly in itself; and the unfortunate candidate, on climbing out, has to make

1. Sanday and Headlam, International Critical Commentary, p. 154; quoted in H. Wheeler Robinson, *The Life and Faith of the Baptists*, Methuen 1927, p. 79. Wheeler Robinson was possibly the greatest of Baptist theologians, certainly in modern times, and I recommend anyone interested in this subject to Section III of his book.

a considerable journey to the nearest vestry door, while enthusiasts swaddle him in warm clothes. On one occasion, as the last banal touch, I saw a cup of steaming cocoa provided.

Vicarage Road was an old-fashioned church with an old-fashioned baptistery. When it was opened, there was a general air as of running repairs going on in the building. But father had a fine touch with a ceremony and I found baptisms fascinating. It was always assumed that at an appropriate age I would be baptized myself, and when I was fifteen I plucked up my courage to go through with it. I am not quite sure about my motives. The hints from my mother, beginning to get embarrassing, that it was time I did? A desire to please my father? A performer's desire to be at the centre of the stage – for a baptism can be high drama, no doubt about that? All these things, perhaps, but there was certainly also some spiritual prompting. I do not think fear had much to do with it, because father was not a hellfire man, in the sense that he never used fear as a weapon with which to make conversions. I was interviewed, as all candidates had to be, by two of the church deacons, since baptism implied becoming a church member. Their cross-examination was not exactly searching, though I do remember one of them saying, 'The church of God is the means by which He is going to save the world, and to join it is the greatest privilege that any human being can have.' But I was not impelled by any desperate feeling of necessity about the Church.

No, I think I simply had a love for the person of Jesus Christ. This was not the same as thinking that he was, as given to us in the records, always right; or accepting any specific theological view as to his nature. But this at least is the beginning of the Christian faith, and for me it has survived the vicissitudes of the years. Later on in life I read a good deal of Christian apologetic, and I have always found Christianity an intellectually adequate faith. But in times of trouble it is the person of Christ, not the theology of Christianity, which offers comfort. So although there was something of the hypocrite about me when I was baptized, as there often has been since, I can say with Paul, 'I know whom I have believed.' An important distinction – not *what* I have believed, but *whom*.

I remember my baptism vividly: the hissing gas lights, the cricket shirt and flannels which I wore, the tension on my father's face when I went down into the waters of Jordan and he took me in his arms; the moment his voice nearly broke, and forgetting the correct procedure of reciting the full names of the candidate, he simply said 'My dear boy Alan . . .' – and then, as I came up, gasping a bit for breath, the surge of song from the congregation.

Just as I am, without one plea,
But that Thy blood was shed for me,
And that thou bid'st me come to Thee,
O Lamb of God, I come!

I shall make a good many references to hymns in the course of this book. They have been one of the principal cultural influences of my life, if one can use the word 'cultural' in this connection. At that time I already had a perception that some hymns were better than others, in more than a subjective sense.

Just as I am, though tossed about
With many a conflict, many a doubt,
Fightings and fears within, without,
O Lamb of God, I come!

These lines comforted Wordsworth's daughter Dora when she was dying. Wordsworth himself could not bear to have them repeated in his presence, which was ungracious of him, since by then he had written whole tracts of far worse stuff himself. Their origin is unromantic. They were written by Charlotte Elliott at Brighton, when she wanted an excuse for not going to a church bazaar. Well, the spirit bloweth where it listeth.

The various psychiatrists who have punctuated my somewhat eccentric adult life have usually been deeply interested in my baptism, and have suggested that it is likely to have set up all kinds of neuroses. I doubt it. If you are brought up a Baptist the thought of believer's baptism is familiar enough. I had watched hundreds before I was baptized myself. It is, however, a sufficiently challenging experience to make a candidate think twice before going through with it, and this is surely all to the good.

My mind moves on to a baptism many years later, at the same Emmanuel Church, Falmouth, where the television programme was to take place. Father was minister there during the war years, and I have in front of me his baptismal register for the year 1940. On 24 October, Eileen Prior, Sylvia Eustice, Muriel Knuckey, Joan Strike, Stella Brice and Fred Christophers were baptized. Father's note in the 'Remarks' column reads: 'Baptized during Air Raid in which enemy plane was hit by AA gun and exploded in the air.' Father often reverted to this baptism of fire as the most dramatic moment in his ministry. I do not suppose the five girls and the boy have forgotten it either. Falmouth was having a rough time, and the noise was tremendous, but almost the entire congregation stayed standing in their places while the baptisms were taking place.

At least twice during childhood I had prolonged moral periods. For months at a time I would not tell or listen to dirty stories, was meticulous in avoiding a lie, and generally must have been a noxious little prig. I would run past public houses, ostentatiously holding my nose. Mother would say proudly (and as it turned out mistakenly) 'Alan will always be a good temperance man!' Not that running past the pubs was altogether foolish, because many of them in Leyton then did smell unpleasantly. One day, coming back from a football match, father and I saw a man carrying away a jug of beer from The Coach and Horses. He dropped the jug, and the beer swilled into the gutter. The look on his face (he was very poorly dressed) was tragic. Father hesitated: should he give him the money to replace it? Impossible thought! We walked on, but father was troubled that evening. So was I, troubled that father should even have contemplated so base an action. This was what I was like in my moral periods. Their worst effect was probably that when I stopped being moral I rebounded too far in the opposite direction.

I have relatively few memories of Sir George Monoux Grammar School, though it was a good school. It had tradition, dating back to the Middle Ages, and James Hilton had been one of its pupils, before he went to the Leys, where he met the original 'Mr Chips'. There was a terrifying gym master, who put us through the most abominable contortions, and my chief concern each week was to find a good excuse for dodging gym. Games, on the other hand, I enjoyed enormously, though I had no particular talent for them. The school was several miles from home, and involved a long journey each way by tram. There were one or two other boys who had to make the same trip, and we took the opportunity of these lengthy periods to discuss the facts of life. I can remember clearly how this custom began – it also brought one of my moral periods to an abrupt end. My neighbour turned to me solemnly, as we were going home one evening, rather with the air of a man taking out his pipe after dinner. 'By the way,' he said conversationally, 'how do they get babies nowadays?' I suppose modern sexual education is sensible, but it does deprive the children of much fascinating speculation. I class this remark with another made a few years later, at boarding school, by our dormitory prefect. 'You know, men,' he told us – we were all several years his junior – 'you know, when I first heard about the facts of life, I didn't believe them. I thought of my parents. I thought of' – he paused for effect – 'Their Majesties King George the Fifth and Queen Mary . . .' And we were silent, wide-eyed in the darkness, taking in the vision.

I did not do very well at Monoux, and in my second year there father decided to send me to a public school. This was a breathtaking prospect. No member of our family on either side had ever been to a public school. I was not clever enough, or had not worked hard enough, to win a scholarship, but at Taunton there was some remission of fees for the sons of Nonconformist ministers (the school was originally the Independent College, Taunton). Even so, it must have been an extraordinary effort on his part to find the money. So in 1936 off I went, and spent the next six years there.

Taunton was not a very good school at that time. The headmaster had been ill, and the place had grown too slack (though I would always prefer, as pupil or parent, a school that is too slack to a school that is too hearty). Donald Crichton-Miller, the new headmaster, arrived the same term as I did. He had a great reputation for dealing with slackers. We first met after ten days, when I had run away and he fetched me back. I had only got as far as Wellington, about seven miles, so it was not a very heroic effort on my part. Crichton-Miller then and thereafter was kindness itself to me, though most people found him a formidable man. His headmastership transformed the fortunes of the school, with some fortuitous help from the fact that there was a war, and we were in an enviably safe area. Nevertheless, my first year away at school was acutely miserable. It was not that there was anything consistently savage about the way I was treated, though I can recall one shocking example of bullying in my own case and several more affecting others. It was simply that I could not adjust myself to being away from home. I begged to be taken away; ran away three times, never getting very far, and on one occasion ran away from home when the time had come to go back to school.

Whether my parents were right to disregard my long-continued pleas and keep me there, trusting that I would ultimately – how I came to hate the phrase – 'settle down', I do not find it easy to say. I doubt if it can ever be justified to inflict the unhappiness on a child that I suffered. On the other hand, I did settle down in the end, and even enjoyed myself. The process of settling down made me a tougher person, which is supposed to be useful in life; also a nastier one, but that may be useful too. Oxford purged some of the nastiness, but not all.

In due course I sent my own children to a public school (though not the same one). I explained to myself that this was only because home life suggested it, and that public schools are very different from what they were (just as they always were). I had always maintained that until middle-class parents sent their children to state schools the state system would not be as good as it should be. Yet I contracted out of the system, just as my father had done before me. The decisive moment was when a friend pointed out that the welfare of one's children was probably more important than one's principles; and that, in any case, my principles seemed to be coinciding neatly with the welfare of my pocket. So off they went.

But it was a real dilemma which I faced, and it was a real, though different, dilemma which my parents must have faced in 1936–7, when every day's post brought from me a passionate plea for release. 'What would *you* have done?' my mother asked me many years later, handing me a letter I had written at that time, which for some macabre reason she had kept. I could not answer. I read no more than the first sentence of the letter, as soon as she turned her back I burned it.

All this sounds ungracious to Taunton School. But it was not the school's fault that I was, in the jargon of the day, a mixed-up kid. It had many fine qualities: excellent drama, and even better music. John Wilkins was responsible for the first, and Arthur Temple for the second. They were both remarkable men, the kind of dedicated schoolmaster who has deliberately spurned richer and more famous opportunities elsewhere. Arthur Temple loved music, loved it carefully and humbly, and he had the ability to communicate his love to his pupils. In the same way, John Wilkins had a quiet passion for drama, and for poetry, which was unforgettable for anyone with the inclination or mental equipment to respond. At one stage of my life I found myself producing, for sound radio, quite large casts of actors, many of them capable and experienced. I had not expected at all to be doing that kind of thing when I joined the BBC. I had no professional training or background for it. So I tried to remember what John Wilkins had done, and I found I got along pretty well.

Every school has somebody approximating to Mr Chips, and at Taunton it was the second master, S. P. Record. He was deaf, and carried a large battery-operated headphone hearing aid around with him. Sometimes he would let the batteries run down, and all that was needed for a Latin or Greek construe was a confident mumble and a knowledgeable air. He had an assortment of nicknames, of which in my time 'Rozz' was the most popular (an abbreviation of 'rozzer', i.e. policeman, which term had been introduced to the school by a drama club production of *The Amazing Dr Clitterhouse*). For such occasions as roll-call he would discard his apparatus, and once the History Sixth responded to the calling of their names with a cry of 'Rozz'. No reaction was provoked until a wretched day boy, holy or scared or both, replied with the conventional '*Adsum*'. The difference between the noises caused Mr Record to tumble to what had been going on (he was shrewd), and the vengeance was considerable. But he bore no malice. He knew the ways of boys and probably even enjoyed the silly joke.

He often preached in the Dissenting chapels in Taunton, not a 'powerful' preacher as the phrase used to go, but thoughtful and penetrating. Despite his deafness, he too had something of the communicating gift of Temple and Wilkins, and could be inspiring on the classics. But, to my lasting regret, I never had much of a classical education. After the Remove (Upper Fourth) we were delivered for Latin and Greek to a hopeless teacher (though he might have made a good don). He had pleasant personal qualities, but not the least notion of teaching boys. There were six of us in his Greek set. All these six later won open awards to universities, in other subjects than the classics. Three of them took first-class honours in their degrees. They were not dull boys. But all six failed to get even a 'weak pass' (33 per cent) in Greek in School Certificate. Our teaching consisted of the man reading to us in translation, with scarcely a word of commentary, the required books of Xenophon and Homer. For a senior master at an expensive public school it was an astonishing performance. I imagine he was getting paid about four times as much as Arthur Bird at Farmer Road.

There were a lot of men at Taunton to whom I have cause to be grateful; but I will only mention two more, because these were the historians. J. F. Elam taught me history from the fifth form, until shortly before I managed, after several unsuccessful attempts, to win an exhibition to Oxford. He could be a harsh critic, and there were times when I hated him. But he was a real historian, and a master of the English language. He detested the over-written, slapdash style to which I was prone: he liked a writer to be judicious and economical in his use of words: but he recognized soon that I too was a historian of sorts, and took much trouble for me.

He left, by a coincidence, to be headmaster of Sir George Monoux Grammar School, and I was nursed up the final slopes by E. L. King, an extraordinary man. He had been to The Queen's College, Oxford, where I was to go myself, and where my sons were to go. 'Oxford's my Mecca,' he would say, with an accent we were always trying to imitate but could never quite achieve. He had just missed a first, and with it I suppose his hopes of becoming a Fellow of Queen's, which he would have liked above all things. He was an enthusiastic musician, with an attractive wife who became stunningly beautiful when she played the violin, which she did extremely well. We used to sing glees in his sitting-room, gazing at Connie: once he was describing how his night's sleep had been interrupted by an air-raid alarm. 'Connie and I leapt out of bed,' he said, 'slipped our pyjamas on . . .' It was no more than a slip of the tongue, but I can recall the awe-stricken faces of the glee group as they envisaged the situation.

Eric King was a devout Christian, much influenced by McEwan Lawson, who spent some years at Taunton as school chaplain. It was McEwan Lawson who persuaded King to preach in chapel, a thing assistant masters rarely did. 'Did you listen to King's sermon?' asked my housemaster at lunch the next day, as between men who normally were forced to *hear* sermons but did not *listen* to them. 'I was amazed,' he went on. 'Amazed. I mean – that's the best sermon that has been preached in that chapel for years.' So it was: about the devil driven out of a man, who returns with seven others worse than himself. It is a hard parable, and I would not risk trying to recall King's treatment of it, except that he used it to illustrate the severe difficulties of self-reformation, and the need for the presence of the Holy Spirit if a room, though swept and garnished, is not to be dangerously empty.

King became a headmaster of a grammar school. He became national chairman of the Student Christian Movement. Finally he became a parson. The last news I had of him, some years ago, was when he was Vicar of Theale. A broadcasting colleague of mine had been to see him. His wife, Connie of the violin and the pyjamas, had apologized for the inadequacy of the hospitality, and he had himself pointed out, ruefully, that they could have done better in past days: 'but the Holy Ghost was too strong, old boy.' To no one who knew him will this remark sound pompous or pretentious. Not long afterwards he died.

For some years after I went to Taunton I was still intending to become a parson myself. My father had never made any attempt to persuade me, one way or the other. He had made sacrifices to give me what he believed to be the best education possible, and I dare say that to become a Baptist minister would have been the greatest reward I could make. So the question arose whether I had a 'vocation'. The word has always been used too glibly. Some people, the fortunate ones or it may be just the good ones, never have any doubt about their calling to the ministry. In spite of much thought, and varyingly conscientious attempts at prayer, I could not be sure whether I had a vocation or not. I sheltered behind the convenient theory that you have to be sure, and by the time I had reached the sixth form I knew the ministry was not for me. I was left, and occasionally still am, with the thought that perhaps I was taking the easy way out, that I could not face the hard work, the footslogging, the miserable salary. But it would be wrong to say that I have ever regretted it. And it did turn out that through religious broadcasting, rather unexpectedly, another way of Christian work was opened.

4 Munich

I was brought up to fear and detest war. My father was, for some years, a pacifist, though he reluctantly decided in 1939 that the war was necessary. Some of the pictures he would draw in his sermons on Remembrance Sunday were as grim as Sassoon or Blunden.

It was thus understandable that early in October 1938 he should begin a letter to me,

> My dear Son,
>
> What a wonderful blessing it is of our Heavenly Father that there should be this settlement at Munich. What hopes it brings of a true and lasting international peace. I thank God for a good man like Neville Chamberlain . . .

Now father was not a Tory. He was a sound Liberal who might have voted Labour if he had no Liberal candidate. Nor did he have any particular admiration for politicians. Even the fact that they were both Baptists did not make it easy for him to approve of Ernest Brown (I wonder how many now recall that pillar of what used to be called the Liberal National party). Sir Cyril Black would have made no appeal to him.

Nevertheless, father saw the hand of God in the Munich settlement. So did I. So, though they might not have put it that way, did nearly everyone at school. What is more, the only ones who disapproved were the blood-and-thunder boys, the bash-the-Jerries, why-isn't-the-corps-compulsory gang. The only intelligent person at school whom I can remember disapproving of Chamberlain at that time was J. F. Elam. He was quietly sardonic about the whole thing, especially Chamberlain's piece of paper, and as a result suffered some unpopularity among the boys and, I suspect, in the masters' common-room. Geoffrey Mander, a few years later, wrote a short book called *We Were Not All Wrong*,[1] which effectively demonstrated that the opposition parties, and especially the Liberal party, had on the whole a good record in foreign affairs in the period 1933–9. But in an election just after Munich they would not, I think, have carried the support even of many traditional followers.

It did not last long. The immediate relief from the menace of mass bombing soon gave way to the thought that it could not be postponed much longer. We spent Christmas at Clacton-on-Sea, where we would sometimes go for a few days' holiday out of season. Many of the details of that holiday come back to me with sharp clarity: especially the train journey on a bitter day over the flat, snow-covered Essex countryside, and the great bowl of hot, steaming stewed steak with which our hostess greeted us when we arrived, hours late. Little things such as that, so often taken for granted, became precious. 'Europe can look forward to a Christmas of peace,' Hitler had said, and somehow his saying of it suggested that it would be the only one for a long time. Father knew by then, as most people did, that Munich had only been at best a delaying action, though he never said as much in front of my mother. The fact that he did so to me I regarded as an important stage in growing up.

That we were in Leyton, in what was expected to be the front line, was an added anxiety to father – not on his own behalf, for he was a brave man, but on mine and particularly mother's. By this time I believe he was feeling that it had been a mistake to go to Leyton at all, that it had not been a true call. We had only been there a few months when mother fell ill of

1. Gollancz, 1943.

consumption. It was usually a killer in 1930, and it was expected to kill her, but since she had an exceptionally tough, though tiny physique she survived; with the generous help of several relations who looked after her for months in the supposedly healthier air of the north of England. I did not realize how ill she was, and the months I spent alone with father, who spoilt me ridiculously, were among the happiest of my life. My mother's illness had possibly been precipitated, or at least her strength lessened, by giving birth to a daughter. Marjorie lived only nine months. A sick wife and a dead daughter were my father's first rewards for going to Leyton.

Mother remained frail for the rest of her life. Father always cleared the grates and laid the fires and brought her breakfast in bed. Things looked up for a while when she came back from the north, but it was proving an unsatisfactory church. This was nobody's fault. The young people were constantly getting married and moving further out, to Buckhurst Hill or Loughton. In one year father baptized thirty new members, and the total church membership was still down at the end of it. There was also a fearful row in the church, of which I picked up information only later and bit by bit. Some of the younger element felt they had a grievance against the deacons. The spark was lit when one venerable deacon got up to speak at the church meeting, and began: 'Sisters and brethren, I am sure the devil is in this house tonight.' The leader of the opposition took it as directly personal (which I dare say it had been meant to be) and stamped out, with his followers.

Father toiled on, bringing in new members, persuading some of the old ones back. After six or seven years he thought he would like a change. He preached 'with a view' at all sorts of places that sounded lovely – Milton-under-Wychwood, I remember, was one. He was repeatedly and inexplicably turned down. After a while it came to his knowledge that he was being turned down because he had a sick wife (some Baptist churches still like to get two people for the price of one). He was furiously angry and nearly gave up his ministry. Mother came in one day, after taking a walk down the pleasances of Leyton High Road, coughing, and asked forlornly, 'What am *I* doing *here*?' I once found father in tears, which happened very rarely (except when he was happy). He preached a little later from the sixth chapter of Isaiah: 'I heard the voice of the Lord, saying, whom shall I send, and who will go for us? Then said I, here am I; send me.' But had God really sent him to Leyton? The old Dissenters were accustomed to look for signs of God's grace, and the witnesses seemed against him.

I would be sorry if any Vicarage Road people who happen to read this misconstrued it. There were some splendid people there; there were many good times. But they were worrying years for my family, made darker by the advancing clouds of war. As it chanced, when war did break out, our own fortunes took a turn for the better. The first evacuation was so comprehensive that father was left virtually without a congregation. He was out of work for some weeks, and then accepted a call to Falmouth, where the minister, a chaplain, had left to join his regiment. Emmanuel was a beautiful, brand-new church, and for five years there father led his happiest and most fruitful ministry. I have seen them, on great occasions, anniversaries or harvest festivals, queuing up for the doors to open at Emmanuel.

Nowadays I would call myself a pacifist. I think I probably was in 1939, but lacked the courage to say so. And yet, like so many other boys of that time, I was moved by the battle in Spain, and had I been a year or two older I dare say I would have volunteered. What nonsense this was! To be willing to fight for Spain in 1938, reluctant to fight for Britain in 1940! I do not try to defend it, but that was the way my emotions pulled. Yet I was anything but a Communist. Since I first became politically conscious I have never doubted that it is right to be a liberal, and also (which certainly might not always be the same thing) a supporter of the British Liberal party.

Yet in that last period before the war, apart from the brief aberration of Munich, there were only two sides in politics. Over Spain one had to declare oneself, much as years later one had to declare oneself over Suez. This was true even at school, and at much more than a cops-and-robbers level. It is not just the modern generation of schoolboys who take politics seriously. We argued incessantly about poverty (of which I had learnt something at Leyton) and, even more, about international affairs. Stephen King-Hall, F. A. Voigt, Vernon Bartlett were the names that punctuated our conversation. I lost a good friend because he was on Franco's side, and he was killed in the second world war before the friendship was mended. This was foolish. As E. M. Forster points out, it is better to betray one's country than to betray one's friend.

A by-product of the Spanish civil war, so far as I was concerned, was that it stimulated my interest in poetry, which so far had not got much beyond Newbolt and Chesterton (not, I am glad to say, that it has ever got 'beyond' Chesterton). I could not for some time make much of Auden, Spender and company, but it did me good to try. For School Certificate we read Milton's shorter poems, but we were so concerned with getting through the examination that we never stopped to think of the poetry. I actually learnt 'Lycidas' by heart without being at all stirred. In the sixth I decided I was not going to bother with Higher Certificate, but would try for an open award at Oxford or Cambridge (there were no other universities then). Freed from syllabuses, I plunged into the Lyrical Ballads. It was joy to have all that poetry to read, and all that time to read it in. I still have copies of some of my essays: not very good, even by schoolboy standards, but breathing a kind of foolish, innocent delight.

If poetry was for fun, history was for work, though that too was often fun, except when Elam insisted on some dry economic subject. At that time it was fashionable in history teaching to say: 'We have bored the wretched children with our kings and prime ministers, battles and treaties: we must excite their interest by teaching them how the common people lived.' For myself, I loved the kings and the battles, and could not abide the Factory Acts and the doctrine of *laissez-faire* (which was what they meant when they talked about how the common people lived). Elam, to be sure, did not subscribe to this nonsense, but felt it necessary to make an occasional gesture towards it. But I was more interested in Sully's Grand Design than his system of taxation. I read Carlyle, not Clapham. The point about Carlyle, and for that matter Macaulay, was that even if they were sometimes wrong they were always readable. When Macaulay published his *History of England* he received a letter from a working-men's club thanking him for writing a history which working men could read. It remains true that if working men cannot read a history book it is not history at all (it might be antiquarianism or archaeology or something like that, but it is not history). It is obviously more important for any historian to be readable than to be right, because if he is not readable nobody will know whether he is right or not – or care. If the price of passing an examination (certainly in history, possibly in anything) is boring yourself stiff, it is better to fail the examination.

In the first months of the war all we embryo historians were busy drawing historical parallels: Britain fighting to preserve the balance of power in Europe, as she had done against Philip of Spain, Louis XIV, Napoleon. The study of history at that time did make it more difficult for us to accept two of the current myths: that all Germans were wicked, and that the French army could not be beaten. We thought it quite likely that France would be beaten, and when she was there was the most terrible rumpus between the Francophiles and the rest. Very wickedly, we played off the sardonic and prophetic Elam against another master who had been passionate in his declaration that 'France will never surrender!' It is not an episode on which I look back with pride, but at least it showed that we were no longer taking things for granted, which is the beginning of wisdom. It was a good form, that History Sixth: as lively a group of minds as I have shared in. But we must have been a headache to our tutors.

After France had fallen our interest in international affairs seemed to evaporate. There was not much we could do, except get on with our work and wait to be called up. For me, the happiest memory of 1940 (apart from falling in love for the first time) was the cricket season. I was appointed to the post of scorer to the 1st XI, and thus for the first time had the blissful experience of travelling round other schools in the West Country, watching cricket all day in the sunshine (it was a good summer), out of class while the others were still at work in the mornings; taking tea on terraces, lunching elegantly in long, cool libraries; making notes about lavatory accommodation. This last unsavoury occupation arose because I was planning a short thesis on the sanitation of our grand old English public schools. It was a project which, like so many others, was never completed, though I revived it briefly some years later when I encountered the hip baths at Trinity, Oxford. One of them would have made a noble frontispiece.

Summer vacation, 1940, at Falmouth was a strange time. One day early in September it was widely believed that the invasion was about to take place, and when I walked into town with father in the morning we were almost the only people in the streets. Barbed wire and concrete blocks on the beaches, Bren and Lewis guns sparsely scattered along the coasts, place names conscientiously removed from public spots . . . At Penmere Platform, the next station before Falmouth on the railway line, the station name was not removed, but turned round to face the other way, presumably on the assumption that the Germans would arrive by train. One could, however, usually find one's bearings by going to the post offices, where in both town and village the names remained in the window for all to see. I walked a lot in west Cornwall that summer, getting to know the county for the first time, and the post offices were sufficient guides. And if they failed, one could turn to the war memorials.

I have never been sure of the accuracy of the traditional picture of a 'phoney' war from September 1939 to the spring of 1940, followed by a mighty girding of the national loins and resurgence of the national spirit. Even at Falmouth, which was often bombed, the war continued to have many comic aspects right through the summer of 1940. Like everyone else, I relished and passed on the rumours that swept the country, especially in the coastal districts, and especially the one about the foiled German invasion and the channel 'white with dead'. I could name three people who personally saw that great tide of corpses. Peter Fleming duly demonstrated that the story was totally groundless, and that even the later theory that a large-scale exercise had been disrupted was untrue.[1] I happened to mention this one day, years later, in Falmouth, and I was

1. His conclusive evidence for this is given in *Invasion, 1940* (Rupert Hart-Davis, 1957).

not only flatly disbelieved but nearly run out of town.

When in 1941 Germany invaded Russia a good deal of political thinking had to be reconsidered. In an excess of enthusiasm a whole school day was set aside for lectures on the Soviet Union. Eric King – who must have spent days mugging up details of Russian industrial progress and the like – lectured the sixth in the morning. In the afternoon someone else explained to us how essentially democratic the Russian constitution was. The evening lecture was given by a somewhat dour character and went as follows: 'I know nothing about Russia. I have read Karl Marx, which is more than most Socialists I know have done, and I regret the time expended. I have something better to read in the next hour, and I hope you have.'

He thereupon sat down. He was in a strong position, as he was about to join the army. We all had to write an essay about Russia, and I denounced Communism at length, saying I considered there was really not much to choose between Stalin and Hitler. In view of my enthusiasm for the Spanish Republicans this was an odd line to take, and I expect I took it only because nobody else did. It got me into some trouble, as I was thought to be insufficiently patriotic. In the public schools in 1941 there was a red in every bed.

I worked quite hard in the sixth, and developed a fluent but highly-coloured English style. My essays would come back marked 'over-written'. Then it occurred to me to place the purpler passages in inverted commas. This worked very well, and the essays would come back marked 'telling quotations'. After being turned down by Cambridge I won my exhibition to Oxford in 1942. I expected to be called up, but as I had a weak chest inherited from mother I was not, and went up to the university in October.

5 Oxford

'Oxford's my Mecca,' was Eric King's phrase: and I could say much the same.

I had four years there. After the first two I was summarily hauled into the army. This was a somewhat discreditable episode which caused my friends considerable mirth then and since, but was not very funny at the time to me. Bored with repeated medical examinations I cut one, for what seemed to me the very good reason that I had a chance to meet C. B. Fry. I omitted to write in advance or apologize afterwards, with the result that one evening I came back to my digs to find two military policemen on the doorstep. The next thing I knew was that I was in the army. As I had been elected President of the Union a short while before, this caused quite a stir.

My military career was brief and unheroic, and spent almost entirely in hospital. After I had been invalided I went back to Oxford for another two years, including one post-graduate. Looking back on this incident I feel I paid pretty heavily for my casualness, as I have never been a really fit man since. In fact I have spent nearly two years of my life in hospital, not counting one spell for a nervous collapse (though that may have had physical origins). But this only gradually became apparent. At the time the months in hospital seemed no more than a tiresome interlude.

Wartime Oxford was a strange but interesting place. Government departments had taken over several of the colleges, including part of Queen's. The city was full of American soldiers (*Punch* published a cartoon of two of them walking down the High, one saying to the other, 'Ah! The

English Detroit'). It was stated that Hitler would never bomb Oxford, since he had decided to make it his English capital, and no bombs fell even at the time of the 'Baedeker' raids. St Peter's Hall was occupied by Westfield, a women's college from London. There were relatively few lectures, though quite a lot of people were still in residence, mostly of course on the scientific side. This shortage of lectures had one odd consequence for me. Since there were no history lectures which it seemed particularly important to attend, I went to none. I did set out for one in the early days, but could not find my way. This became, before long, a habit; by the end of a year it had almost become a fetish. At any rate, after four full academic years, I could lay my hand on my heart and solemnly swear that I had never once been to a lecture. I have never met anyone else who could say this. I have known the boast made, but when pressed it always turned out that those making the claim had succumbed once or twice in the early weeks, or had not survived at the university long.

I mention this as a curiosity, not a matter of pride. There were certainly some lectures, especially in the post-1945 period, which I could usefully have attended. But it does suggest that the importance of lectures is exaggerated. I was fortunate in my tutors, read most of the books I was advised to read and a good many more which I came across myself. The best way to get a degree is still to 'read' for it. I only just scrambled a first after a fairly agonizing *viva voce*, but that was as much as I could have hoped to do anyway, lectures or no lectures. I liked working alone and at hours to suit myself. I would have hated the seminarial system of a group of students working together. But I can only speak for the study of history. Other subjects no doubt require different disciplines.

Post-war Oxford was fascinating. I doubt if the university, so far as the student body is concerned, has ever been richer.

It covered a very broad cross-section of society, from the eighteen-year-old just up from school to the tough colonel or commander (and sometimes private or AB) who had been through six years of war. The usual ferment of ideas, the endless undergraduate talk, was leavened by a deeper experience than usual. Some of the warriors found it difficult to readjust themselves, and hit the gin bottle, but not many. Kenneth Tynan and Henry Fairlie were writing in the university periodicals. M. P. Donnelly, H. A. Pawson, A. H. Kardar were to be seen in the Parks; B. H. Travers, J. O. Newton-Thompson, D. W. Swarbrick at the Rugby ground in Iffley Road, R. G. Bannister at the running track next door.

In the years when I was at Oxford the best mind in the Union, I think most contemporaries would have agreed, was that of Edward Boyle, whom I once called 'the Society's shaggy dog', and who used to while away dull debates by detecting correlations and discrepancies between the first and second prayer-books of Edward VI. The most effective public speakers, probably, were Godfrey Le Quesne, Anthony Crosland and Anthony Wedgwood Benn. Curiously, in the light of later events, we thought of Tony Benn as the safe middle-of-the-road Labour man, and Tony Crosland as the dangerous radical. There was another man full of promise on the Labour side, a speaker of wit and punch, J. A. F. Pickford, who became President, but who soon afterwards died tragically, under the anaesthetic for a trivial operation. The recollection will still give many a twinge of sadness.

In one aspect the wartime period was superior to its successor: poetry. Oxford had at least three outstanding poets (not war poets, primarily) and oddly enough they were all Queensmen. The best was Sidney Keyes, and it took no great perception even then to be sure that his reputation would prosper. He was said to have written 'Remember Your

Lovers' in the examination schools after he had finished his paper. He seems even more relevant now than he did then.

> Walking among this island
> People inhabiting this island city,
> Whose coast recedes, whose facile sand
> Bears cold cathedrals restively:
> I see a black time coming, history
> Tending in footnotes our forgotten land.

Keyes I never met. His friend Drummond Allison, a good poetic craftsman but without the touch of genius, I did know a little, and a charming person he was in the best sense of that rather debased word. Keyes and Allison were both killed in the war. The third of the trio, John Heath-Stubbs, is with us still, and in those days I knew him well.

'Gaunt' is the apt if obvious word to use to describe John. He was well over six feet, very thin, with more bones crammed into his skin than one had thought the human body contained, and all of them jutting out at odd angles. He was nearly blind, and took a first in schools despite having to dictate his papers. It was one of the sights of Oxford to see him progress down the High. He found that if he walked slowly people bumped into him. This irritated them, and restricted his progress. He therefore moved in a series of sprints of about twenty yards, working on the principle that they would get out of his way. Given a sufficiently broad pavement, the hazards were not too bad. For about this distance he would race with enormous strides, scattering everything before him. Then, dyspnoea setting in, he would come to an abrupt halt, and take a book from his pocket. He had, of course, to hold it very close to his eyes. Thus he would stand in the middle of the pavement until he got his breath back, and then he would be away again. Sometimes he would grow interested in his book, forget where he was, and stand there for half an hour or more, a tall lonely rock towering above the waves of humanity which lapped him on every side.

I owe to John Heath-Stubbs my most hilarious experience of the drama. He was the president of the Eglesfield Players, the college dramatic society, and decided that we should produce, as our termly offering, Tourneur's *The Revenger's Tragedy*. The last known production, or so we believed, had been in the reign of Charles I. This Jacobean drama is mostly about a character called Vindice, a kind of madder Hamlet. A wicked duke has murdered Gloriana, Vindice's sweetheart, and Vindice sets out to avenge himself. He does this by arranging a rendezvous between the duke and a lovely lady. The lovely lady is a dummy, topped with Gloriana's skull, and when the duke meets her in a shady bower he is poisoned, because Vindice, the dashing lad, has covered these lips of bone with a dreadful and almost immediate poison. Well, most of the play was like that, but it also includes passages of noble poetry. I was Vindice. I think I originally had 867 lines to learn: I say 'originally' because a large number of cuts had to be made if the play was to be performed in public, as standards of censorship then went. I was rather relieved about the cuts, on more grounds than one. I can still recall the opening lines. When the curtain rose I was discovered, clad throughout in black, holding Gloriana's skull. It was a real skull. There were sounds of revelry off stage. I was to say,

> Duke! Royal lecher! Go, grey-hair'd adultery!
> And thou his son, as impious steep'd as he:
> And thou his bastard, true-begot in evil:
> And thou his duchess, that will do with devil –
> Four excellent characters!

But before I had got beyond the 'Duke!' everyone started

laughing. They laughed and laughed and laughed, just at me standing there with Gloriana's skull. All the earnest women who had come because it was English literature, all the dons of Queen's who were being loyal, the *Oxford Mail* reporter; Nevill Coghill, A. L. Rowse, John Wain: how they laughed, the wretched groundlings.

We brought down the house again in the second act. John Heath-Stubbs himself had been playing the part of the Judge, who only appears in the earlier scenes. This duty done, he undressed so far as his waist; something diverted his attention, and he forgot to do anything about dressing again. He started wandering about to see how things were going and, short-sighted as he was, strayed on to the stage. His appearance was greeted by cheering as loud as if Oxford had scored a try at Iffley Road.

Then there was the episode of Henry Pullinger, though this was only appreciated in its full beauty by members of the cast. *The Revenger's Tragedy* has a large cast, and sundry characters not normally dramatically inclined had to be brought in to help. Henry Pullinger was captain of college cricket and rugby, and batted well against Cambridge at Lord's in a crisis. He is, I am confident, a sound geographer, a subject which he now teaches at Clifton. Acting was not his métier. He nevertheless rallied round in the emergency, and was cast for the role of Second Noble. In our abbreviated version of the play he had only one line. The dialogue goes as follows:

Lussurioso: . . . A blazing star!
First Noble: A blazing star, O, where, my Lord?
Lussurioso: Spy out.
Second Noble: See, see, my Lords, a wondrous dreadful one!

A powerful line, certainly. But at the dress rehearsal Henry could not remember it. There was a pause of agony, punctuated only by John Heath-Stubbs, in the stalls, uttering in a ferocious undertone 'Idiot! Idiot! Idiot!'

Upon the day itself Henry determined that no such calamity should occur. He carefully wrote out 'See, see, my Lords, a wondrous dreadful one' on a piece of paper, a very small piece of paper, which he then gummed to the palm of his hand. This had the effect of ruining his gesture: he was supposed to point at the star, but was unable to do so, since he had to curve his palm towards himself. He normally wore glasses but these had been sternly prohibited. However, bringing his hand close to his forehead, as though in intense pain, Henry managed to get out his line of immortal verse. I think that by that time John had gone over to the Lamb and Flag.

The cuts we made in the play seem surprising now. As I look over my marked copy, I see the loss of one rather pleasing line:

> How dost, sweet musk-cat,
> When shall we lie together?

And this –

> For indeed a bastard by nature should make cuckolds
> Because he is the son of a cuckold-maker

– was thought unfit for public performance. Yet despite our precautions Mrs Hodgkin, the wife of the Provost of Queen's, swept out before the end, thus drawing another hearty burst of applause from the audience.

Yet, Lord! there was some poetry in it; and no acting career, however brief, can have been altogether barren given the chance of speaking such lines as these:

And now methinks I could e'en chide myself
For doating on her beauty, though her death
Shall be reveng'd after no common action.
Does the silkworm expend her yellow labours
For thee? For thee does she undo herself?
Are Lordships sold to maintain Ladyships
For the poor benefit of a bewildering minute?
Why does yon fellow falsify highways,
And put his life between the judge's lips,
To refine such a thing; keeps horse and men
To beat their valours for her?
Surely we are all mad people, and they
Whom we think are, are not . . .

I like to think I spoke the lines well, though I doubt if they had much meaning for me. At that time I was still cocksure about such things as right and wrong, and black and white, and madness and sanity.

At Oxford one begins to make friendships. School friendships usually fade. You meet one another twenty years on, and wonder rather embarrassedly what you can have had in common. But many university friendships can be let alone for years, and picked up on meeting as fresh as when they were set down. To be sure, one of my warmest friends at Oxford was Roger Hedley Miller, with whom I had also been at school. Golf was his passion. This is a game I have never played; but Roger introduced me to the writings of Bernard Darwin, which have always been a delight to me, whether about golf or anything else.

We had a common interest in music: not long ago I was listening to a performance of 'Israel in Egypt', and up came that valiant duet for tenor and bass, 'The Lord is a Man of War'. Now Roger and I had been accustomed to sing this, with all the welter of 'pom-POMs' for the organ bits, on every possible occasion. We both had loud and resonant voices. Many is the cricket team returning from an away match that has suffered from us. Many is the common room or pub that quailed and emptied as we reached the tricky middle bit. I was moved to ring him up the same evening and we talked happily as familiar friends do, and even tried a few of the simpler passages. This is an illustration of picking up friendships as happily as one has set them down. Roger Hedley Miller read forestry, improbable as that sounds as an Oxford subject, and married a girl on whom I had been very keen myself. He had a head of red hair which stuck up vertically, and had been appropriately known at school as 'Busby'. When he left school, his house (for he was head of a house) presented him with an inscribed cigarette case. The occasion was unusual: few hungry schoolboys would dig so deeply into their pockets. The gift itself, in the circumstances, was equally unusual, and must have caused Eric King (who was housemaster) some careful theological thought.

But most of my Oxford friends were newly acquired, and many of them were Liberals (not Roger, a crusted Tory at eighteen). It is not necessary, indeed it is a damnable heresy, that to be friends with a man, or woman, you should share the same political beliefs. But Liberalism was important to me, and there was a lot to do, so it was inevitable that young Liberals should be a good deal in one another's company.

My first act of political campaigning had been in 1929 at Ilkley. I persuaded mother to write a handsome placard in yellow crayon, 'Vote for Holdsworth', and stick it on my toy car, in which I then paraded up and down Middleton Road. (At that time it was considered perfectly proper for a Nonconformist minister not to hide his politics, so long as they were Liberal.) I was deeply disappointed when Holdsworth was bottom of the poll; though had I known it, even worse was to follow, for he ultimately got himself elected for another constituency as a Liberal National.

Then I was agent for the Liberal candidate in a form election at Monoux (bottom of the poll again) but otherwise took no active interest in party politics (as opposed just to politics) until I reached Oxford. There I subscribed my half-crown to the Liberal Club on the first evening, and was happily involved with it for so long as I was up.

I think it is fair to say that the Oxford Liberals in my years were an able and distinguished lot. Most of them have remained Liberals, and most of them would have achieved political office had they not chosen to remain within an unsuccessful party. A good many of them were Queensmen. We provided the President for term after term, and at one stage over half the college were members of the Liberal Club. But there were plenty from other colleges. I remember particularly that Westfield, the evacuated women's college from London, provided redoubtable support, including Betty Evans, who was the first woman undergraduate to speak from 'the paper' at the Union. Among the Liberals of this time I recall Basil Wigoder, John Baker, John Long (a scientific Methodist able in all things but guile), Robert Shackleton (Bodley's Librarian), Kenneth Lamb, who became the BBC's Secretary, and Henry Fairlie (one that rather noticeably got away). Henry I have seen only rarely since then, but I think he is the most exclusively political animal I have ever met. A few years ago I mentioned to him that I thought John Arlott was the best radio cricket commentator. Henry immediately bridled, and said, 'You only say that because he's a Liberal.'

Jeremy Thorpe was a few years after me at Oxford. I first met him during the general election of 1951. He was still reading for the bar, and was not a candidate, but toured the south-western divisions, speaking (sizing them up, too, I dare say, as to future possibilities). I was chairman of the Totnes Liberal Association (the local association, not the divisional one). That election was the worst the Liberals have had. We had asked for trouble the year before, by fighting a vast number of hopeless seats, and losing hundreds of deposits. In Totnes, while we were not much worried about the deposit, we knew our vote would drop – though we had a good candidate, H. E. Desch, fighting for the second time. We knew that Jeremy had been President of the Oxford Union, and were pleased that he came to speak for us, but when I saw him, bowler hat and stick and fancy waistcoat, I wondered how he would come to terms with a Devon audience. I felt no more confident when he started to tell funny stories in a Devon accent.

Jeremy is such a good mimic that even his enemies rarely risk deriding the talent. I have heard him give an impression of a conversation among the members of the Foot family, and you always knew which Foot was which when Jeremy was doing it, more than you could sometimes say when the Foots themselves were. It is not that Jeremy caricatures his subjects – the slightest emphasis of carefully observed mannerisms makes his point.

That said, in 1951 he had not quite mastered the Devon inflections, or at least the South Devon inflections; and yet in no time at all he had mastered his audience. They laughed at every joke, nodded at every profundity, clapped and cheered him and asked for his autograph. I am not sure that I liked him very much on that first occasion. I expect I was jealous, because I was supposed to be the local bright young Liberal, and no pig likes being out-acorned under his own oak. We all knew, however, that the party had a major acquisition. Nor did it ever occur to me, then or thereafter, that we might lose him, even though it was a time when we were losing many bright young men.

I saw a good deal of Jeremy in the next decade, through politics and also through broadcasting, and I am proud of his friendship. I had no doubt that in due course he would, and should, lead the party. Perhaps in the event it came to him a little too soon, but that was hardly his fault. There have been occasions, not many, in his years of leadership when I have felt him mistaken – less in his own judgement than in yielding to party pressures. But it is hard for a relatively young leader to assert himself in an argumentative, not to say eccentric company, and in any case he is not, thank goodness, dictatorial by temperament. I did not share the criticisms made of him after the elections of 1974. Nobody else could have done as well. He converts people, and I am one of the faithful.

I would like in passing to salute another friend of mine over the years, Tim Keigwin, who was the Conservative candidate for North Devon, against Jeremy, in a series of elections, once coming hair-raisingly close to beating him. I met Tim through the West of England programme 'Sports Page', to which he would contribute, admirably, racing reports. Often we would meet in the Exeter studios, when perhaps he had been to Haldon and I to the County Ground for Rugby. Afterwards we would talk, politics among other things, over a beer or two in the Royal Clarence Hotel, a lovely building in the cathedral close. Our talk was always amicable, although Tim is a man of the Right – so far right, Jeremy once said, that he was out in the North Sea. Tim was once asked, in an interview, whether he was a 'Powellite', and replied, carefully, 'No, I am not a Powellite, because *he* is an abolitionist.' It would have been interesting to see Tim in Parliament, and I hope he gets there one day – though not for North Devon.

I nearly stood for parliament for the Liberals in 1945. I was adopted for the Duddeston division of Birmingham, but we did not go to the polls. We discovered, too late, that the £150 deposit had to be paid in cash. But I did a lot of speaking in that election, and enjoyed everything except the result: except perhaps one meeting on the eve of poll, or nearly, at Nailsworth. I had been told to hold the floor for our candidate, Mr Peter Cadbury ('Cadbury for Quality! Cadbury for Stroud!') and after I had been going for half an hour, the audience getting restive, was handed a note saying 'Please explain to the audience that Mr Cadbury will not be able to turn up.' I was not lynched, but Peter Cadbury did not win the seat.

Not that he would have done anyway: yet in 1945 quite a lot of people believed in a major Liberal revival. It was commonly predicted in the newspapers that we would win forty or fifty seats. There was a campaigning song (always grisly things in retrospect) which went,

'Violet Bonham Carter's lot can never hope for fame!'
So the hopeful Tories said – it seemed a likely claim –
But, alas! they quite forgot to reckon with the Dame
Leading the Liberal Revival!

Violet Bonham Carter was the president of the party at that time. When the election was all over, Quintin Hogg observed mordantly, '*De mortuis nil nisi bonum carter.*'

I have never believed since in a Liberal 'revival' – in the sense that I have never expected a general election to bring us any dramatic gains, never expected that we should, as I once heard Clement Davies say (and how we cheered!) 'sweep the country'. Equally, I have never had any doubt that it was right to do what one could to keep the Liberal party in being.

My reasons for this have been, I suppose, religious. That is to say, I would not have been an active Liberal had I not been a kind of Christian. It does not follow that all Liberals should be Christians, or *vice versa*: but this was my own interpretation of belief, and no man can do more than make his own humbly and in goodwill. But religious beliefs apart, what is a man to do if he is on the 'left' in politics, a 'progressive' (I put the words in inverted commas because they are vague but must for the moment serve) – and yet if he thinks that socialism is economic bosh? Where else is that man to go? Dingle Foot was one of many who believed that the Labour party could be liberalized. I suppose the Labour party has become less socialist over the years (though not in theory), but it has simultaneously become much less liberal. Liberals who try to liberalize the Labour party end with all the drab dogma of socialism and none of its love, or else get too old and tired to bother any more. Equally, Liberals who join the conservative party (though it is difficult to think of a true Liberal who has) end up as conservatives, valiantly displaying their radical views by voting against the death penalty once every five years.

This was what I thought in Oxford days, and it is what I think now. If the Liberal party had not existed, I would have had to invent it. And this is what most Liberals feel, which is why the Party continues to survive, although it has been so often left for dead. Nor is Liberal activity useless, even if direct power is remote. It is important to keep together a body of progressive, non-socialist opinion. We give the others most of their good ideas. At the time of the Yellow Book in the late twenties someone said that the once great Liberal party had become 'a university for politicians', and Ramsay Muir observed that even if that were true it was not a dishonourable fate. The first by-election in which I ever spoke was at Berwick, on behalf of Sir William Beveridge. In 1951 we were warning of the dangers inherent in the Central African Federation. In

1959 my own executive in the Falmouth/Camborne division asked me to 'go steady' on the Common Market, which at that time we were the only party to support, and it might have made a big and beneficial difference to the country's future had we seriously set about joining Europe in 1959. Most Liberal attitudes have been justified over the years. Fewer people can now be found to defend the Suez war than the Munich peace. *Apartheid* looks no lovelier than it did in 1960, in which year I declined to broadcast commentaries on the South African rugby team.

Whatever may be the future of the Liberal party, there has been a substantial advance since 1951. After that election I thought we were finished. I was quite prepared to go down with the ship, but I thought it was sinking. At that time we were reduced to six members (later it became five) and of those only Jo Grimond won in a three-cornered fight. The gains since then, in parliament, in the popular vote, and in local government, have been much more than could reasonably have been hoped, and I am very glad to have had a small part in the process.

Despite some obvious outward differences, there were similarities between the young Liberals of Oxford in 1942–7 and those of today. We were the liveliest and most unconventional of the political clubs. We even chalked slogans on walls, not in those days considered a Liberal activity. The day before Lady Violet Bonham Carter's visit to the club, Henry Fairlie and Ian Whyte, our two heroes of Corpus, slunk out at night and in prominent places throughout the city wrote 'Liberalism Lives!' 'Liberalism Thrives!' and – the master touch, we felt – 'LIBERALISM AD LIB!' We wore corduroy trousers instead of jeans. Dirndl skirts were not so relentlessly aggressive as minis, but provided a fair show in a high wind or swinging round at a dance. I once saw a girl fall into the river and her frock made a pattern round her head like a gorgeously coloured water-lily. If the undergraduates were a quieter lot than usual, it was still a youthful society, full of immature enthusiasms. I sometimes think today that we describe a person as mature when all that has happened is that he has grown dull. F. W. Boreham, the Australian preacher, described how in middle age he read again some of the sermons he had written as a young man. He was disconcerted to find that nearly every paragraph began with 'O!' 'O, my friends . . .!' 'O, my brethren . . .' *et alia*. Then he reflected that he wished he could still, in maturity, cry out 'O!' in his sermons with all the confidence and passion that had been his in youth.

I remember one particular demonstration, at Queen's, in which I was involved. The college had achieved four bumps in the summer eights, an almost unbelievable achievement, since we had never been much of a rowing college (though a few years later we did go head of the river). Bump suppers had been reintroduced by most colleges, but the Provost of Queen's, Sir Oliver Franks, felt that they were inappropriate to a period of austerity, and refused permission. I led a deputation to him, but we found him adamant. Junior college was indignant. On the Saturday evening, when the trumpet blew (Queen's is summoned to dinner by a trumpet, as laid down by its founder, Robert Eglesfield) all the student body stood with bowed heads in their places while an oar, draped in black, was ceremonially carried into hall and laid at the foot of high table. Silence was then observed throughout dinner. It was broken at the end by three cheers for the Boat Club, after which we all left. As student demonstrations went even then, this seemed to me a dignified affair. It was an uncharacteristic thing for Franks to do. He was a great and popular Provost, but we found him that day in a Crippsian mood.

The dons presented Oxford's customary rich variety. Doubtless some of them deliberately cultivated their reputations as eccentrics. There was one (not at Queen's) who was in the habit of crawling round the room on all fours while his pupils read their essays. A lady student with particularly succulent ankles might, it was said, tempt him to take a passing bite. Of this same man it was told that a student (male) entered his rooms and found the sitting-room vacant. He was hailed by a distant voice, and perceived through the open door his tutor in the bedroom, sitting on a pot. 'Sit down,' he was instructed in the familiar nasal boom. 'Read me your essay.' The essay was read, the tutor unmoving. There was a pause. 'Very well. You may go now.' And then, as the pupil was leaving, the voice boomed again. 'Perhaps before you go, you will hand me your essay in here. I have a very good use for it.' I do not vouch for this story. I suspect that some of the stories told of Oxford dons are as old as the university, and Oxford has been there a long time: though not quite so long as University College believed when they celebrated the thousandth anniversary of their foundation by Alfred the Great, and the Regius Professor of History, as his contribution to the festivities, sent along a burnt cake.

At Queen's we still had T. W. Allen, a white-haired patriarch with a magnificent-looking head. He was very old, and would progress with the utmost stateliness round the cloisters, pausing every few yards to utter a resounding, trumpet-like cough: 'grrrrrrWOOFWoofwoffumpumpump.' He was known, not unfittingly, as 'God', believed to be because he had once, while reading the lessons in chapel, begun: 'And God said . . . grrrrrrWOOFWoofwoffumpump-ump.' When I first went up my principal tutor was Norman Sykes. It was said that he had his eye on a bishopric, and that his conversation was punctuated with remarks such as

'Salisbury's not very well, you know'; and 'I understand there are signs of decay in Bath and Wells'. I cannot say I remember this myself. I liked Sykes, and kept in touch with him in later years. He became Dean of Winchester, but soon afterwards died, suddenly and far too soon. Only a week or two later we were scheduled to take part in a broadcast together. He was a Yorkshireman, and devoted to cricket. If he never became a bishop, he received an honour which must have delighted him almost as much. In the year 1954 the cricketers of England were rent (or at least the pressmen of England decided they should be) as to who should lead the side to Australia: Len Hutton, the professional and the man in charge, or David Sheppard, the elegant amateur. The whole question, in retrospect, seems a little comic; not least in that Sheppard, later to become for MCC such a black sheep, was then their white-headed boy. It seemed important at the time, and Norman Sykes acted as intermediary between the two men.[1] For a Yorkshireman, here were indeed the corridors of power.

When, after the war, Sykes had departed to Cambridge, I came under the care of J. O. Prestwich. He had returned from the army to resume charge of history at Queen's, of which he is now Senior Fellow. Prestwich is a man of deep scholarship, an excellent tutor though not of the fashionable kind, even then. He did not rush into print with half-formed conclusions. His pupils could not wave his books about in shiny dust-jackets, subtly conveying that *they* were responsible for that remarkable insight on page 83. Perhaps he went too far in the other direction. He was so anxious to master every detail of a subject, to explore the remotest corners of research, that his scholarship is still not adequately represented in print. I do not suppose this worries him in the least, but it is a pity. I wish he would remember what happened to Acton, to

1. See Sheppard's account in *Parson's Pitch*, Hodder & Stoughton, 1964.

be sure a much more amateur historian but not an undistinguished one. When Acton died he left a great mass of notes for his authoritative *History of Liberty*, but they were no use to anyone else, especially as no one could read his writing. So all we have to remember Acton by is a few volumes of lectures and essays.

Prestwich was a medievalist; so was Billy Pantin of Oriel, another under whom I sat. He had the untidiest rooms in the university, and if it happened that he wanted to refer to a book, or a paper, he would get down on his knees and burrow like a mole, throwing back debris over both shoulders. A kind man, he disliked being severe with even the most casual essay, and after making the necessary corrections and additions would always end with the same phrase: 'But on the whole you've worked that out well.' Someone must have told him of this little habit, or perhaps it was a student who forestalled him (a plan often discussed) by saying, 'Would you say I had worked that out well, sir?' At any rate he became conscious of it, but was still unable to break himself of it. Tutorials would be extended well beyond the scheduled period, while he thought of more and more things to say before the moment of dismissal was upon him. And then, very pink in the face, sometimes glaring at his shirt-buttons and sometimes grinning fiercely at the ceiling, he would get out the hallowed phrase; and then dash for his bedroom door as if the house was on fire, tripping over the *Transactions of the Royal Historical Society* on the way.

Towards the end of my time at Oxford, junior college gave a party to some of the dons, an event which I remember because one of the senior members was introduced to pipe-cleaners. He had been having trouble with his pipe, and somebody offered him a cleaner. He was intrigued, and had to have the workings of the intricate machine explained to him in detail. This done, he plunged the woolly rod into the stem of his pipe, and after a considerable time it emerged at the other end, richly brown, sodden, reeking. He was delighted. He made as if to throw the pipe-cleaner into the fire, but then checked, and turned to the person who had lent it to him: 'But you'll want this back?'

My sons tell me that in their time they had to apologize to their more proletarian friends for being at Oxford at all. Sussex, or Essex, or Wessex are apparently the only respectable places to be. I do not doubt that many of the newer universities are doing things which Oxford is not, and probably could not. But an Oxford degree is still as good as most, and when I go there I find that the quality of life, the blend of tradition and irreverence, is still something to be savoured. I have always wanted my own children to go there, not I think for any snobbish reasons, nor from any belief in Oxford's academic superiority, but simply because I enjoyed myself so much.

6 Devon

After I came down from Oxford, in 1948, I found a job on the extra-mural staff of University College, Exeter (as it then was). This involved lecturing to groups of adult students in the South Devon area. It was a splendid job for a young man. At that time there was still post-war optimism in the air, with numbers of people even in the obscure villages determinedly putting the world to rights, and seeing in evening classes one way of going about it. Since those days adult education has become far more efficiently organized, and far more productive of real academic work (especially in such a subject as local history). But it has also – at least in my experience – become duller. It was a good feeling to go to a village such as Stokenham, in the heart of the South Hams, on a bitter winter's night (travelling by bus, too, until I managed to buy a second-hand Austin Seven) and talk in the schoolroom to perhaps a dozen people about the Reformation or the Industrial Revolution or Napoleon. I was an enthusiast, and so were most of the people in the classes.

Whether I would have been so enthusiastic doing the same work in another place is doubtful. The South Hams of Devon is very beautiful. The coast is stark and grand, save for a few untrustworthy bays; inland all is gentleness – warm, rolling country; red earth; few main roads; venerable churches and farmhouses; estuaries filtering lazily up through the fields till they meet the brisk, crooked little rivers hurrying down from the moors; kind people, good pubs. I soon got to know the by-roads so well that I did not need to travel much on the main roads, and Devon country lanes in spring are all that anyone has ever written about English country lanes. The banks are too high for a view, which is just as well considering the need for careful driving, but at short intervals a gate or a gap gives a sudden prospect, always changing, always inviting. Even the main roads were quiet, then, for we still had petrol rationing (but plenty of coupons went with my work). Perhaps the distance of time enchants the view, but I would still say I have known no lovelier countryside, not even the Yorkshire dales nor the Cotswolds.

I cherish specially some evenings spent at Aveton Gifford, a village two or three miles west of Kingsbridge. The villagers called it 'Avverton Gifford', with a hard G. The gentry and the educated insisted on calling it, with a casual flourish, 'Awton Jifford'; believing that they were getting closer to the soil, no doubt. (Just the same thing, I later discovered, used to happen with the pronunciation of Cirencester.) My class at Aveton Gifford, like everything else in the village, fell under the general direction of the Rector, the Rev. W. A. Pierrepont Dawson. Piers was a splendid man. He always asked me to dinner beforehand, and afterwards we usually talked late. By the last glass we had invariably reached theology. He was very spiky, to use his own word for high church beliefs, and I used to quote to him the parody of Montgomery's hymn –

> And nightly pitch my moving tent
> A day's march nearer Rome

but in fact he remained an Anglican, until his early death. A tall, broad man, with his flowing cassock and wide black hat, as he strode round the lanes he had more the air of a medieval friar than a modern country parson.

Two members of Piers's flock were the Brigadier and his wife. Coming to the study of history comparatively late in life, the Brigadier attacked it with gusto, and every discussion group was enlivened by his forthright views. A subject had no appeal to him unless you could take sides on it, and often the side he adopted was unexpected. The Brigadier could no longer live in the style to which he was accustomed, but refused to give in. One evening my wife and I were asked to his cottage for dinner. There was no butler, so the Brigadier performed the function himself, expertly. At the end of dinner the ladies left, a partition being drawn across the little sitting-room so that the gentlemen could drink their glass of port in peace. When the time came to go, my wife was led off to the ladies' lavatory, and the Brigadier beckoned to me to follow him. We went into the back garden. 'I'm afraid,' he said, 'we don't run to a separate gentlemen's lavatory here; but this is a very good rose bush.'

Another example of the old school was Lady Clementine Waring, of Salcombe. She was a daughter of the tenth Marquess of Tweeddale, and married Walter Waring, MP, who had died in 1930. Although Walter Waring did not hold high political office himself, he was close to the centre of affairs, an intimate of the mighty. This, and her own aristocratic origins, to say nothing of her vivacity and charm, assured Lady Clementine of a place in high Edwardian society. To meet her was to be reminded of that society's gaiety and graciousness. To visit her was like stepping into a story by Saki.

She lived at 'The Moult', a fine house set upon one of the handsomest stretches of the coast. James Anthony Froude had lived there. Your room was a sitting-room as much as a bed-room, with a deep armchair and an antique escritoire, supplied with the notepaper of the house. A dressing-room adjoined for the convenience of your valet. Once I was the only guest, and after dinner Lady Clementine duly departed, and again I was served with port, solitarily. At eleven in the morning the butler would appear with a glass of madeira and a small slice of madeira cake.

When I signed the visitors' book Lady Clementine showed me some earlier volumes, bursting with the great names of the first quarter of the century: David Lloyd George, Winston Churchill, Herbert Henry Asquith. She did this not from pride, but because she knew I would be interested. She was not preoccupied with the past. All her life she was active in all sorts of useful causes – I met her through her interest in adult education. She was proud of the house and its setting, and she drew my attention to a passage which Froude had written about it:

> I have just come in from the terrace. The moon is full over the sea, which is glittering as if it was molten gold. The rocks and promontories stand out clear and ghostlike. There is not a breath to rustle the leaves or stir the painted wash upon the shore. Men and men's doings, and their speeches and idle excitement, seem all poor, transient and contemptible. Sea and rocks and moonlight looked just as they look tonight before Adam sinned in Paradise.

Tennyson visited Froude at Salcombe, and it was watching the waves break over the sand-bar outside the harbour that prompted him to write 'Crossing the bar'. So Lady Clementine averred, and though most of the books say it was written while crossing the Solent, Salcombe seems a likelier inspiration.

Lady Clementine lived to the age of 84. A few days before her death, in 1964, the Salcombe Urban District Council had before it a proposal for residential development on the headland where The Moult stands, but mercifully turned it down. That same year died another indomitable character, who lived in very different circumstances not far away, Miss Elizabeth Prettyjohn of Hallsands. The village of Hallsands, near Start Point, faces due east. For many generations the houses, perched at the brink of the sea, were protected from the strong easterly gales by a bulky pebble beach. In the 1890s the Admiralty was extending Keyham dockyard, and gave permission to the contractor to take the pebbles away. He removed 650,000 tons, lowering the level of the beach by an average height of twelve feet, and in some places as much as twenty feet. In 1900, when the dredgers had worked their way within the high water mark, the villagers began to protest. They kept on protesting, with no effect. On New Year's day 1902 the fishermen gathered on the cliff and refused to allow the mooring rope of the dredger to be fastened to the shore. But by that time the damage was done. The next gale swept away a cottage. Seven more went in the next week. The road collapsed. After every tide the villagers tried desperately to plug the gaps with stones, furze, timber, anything they could find, standing deep in the water to do it. The Admiralty recognized its liability to the extent of subscribing £1500 to the cost of a new sea wall. This was not munificent. A public subscription raised much more. It was too late, and in 1916 a heavy storm swept away nearly all that was left of the village. A new Hallsands was built on top of the cliffs – sad, safe houses, a high price to pay for the obduracy of a jack-in-office in Whitehall, too busy to take notice of silly crab-fishermen.

Elizabeth Prettyjohn, however, refused to move up the cliff. She and her brother stayed on in the one surviving cottage at the sea's edge. In 1962 her brother died, and Miss Prettyjohn was the only inhabitant of old Hallsands. The next gale, or the next, or the next after that, must surely bring the cottage tumbling down and toss her into the sea. She did not need to go on living there: her family and friends were only too anxious to take her away. Indeed, it was difficult to be sentimental about her. She was conscious of her position as the last survivor, and must have done quite well out of the visitors, who came in calm weather to the deserted village, and to whom she would tell an increasingly erratic version of the tragic story. I last met her in 1963, and she was shrewd in negotiating a fee before allowing us to film her. Nevertheless, to think of that huddle of crumbling stones where she lived, and to think of the towering might of a black easterly in Start Bay . . . an awkward, perverse old woman, who caused a lot of people a lot of trouble: but a proper daughter of Devon.

When I go back to the South Hams of Devon now, I notice the changes. But its geographical position, and the quiet, resolute character of its people, keep much of the old character. Perhaps the worst of the onslaughts from upalong came in 1943–4, when there was what is still known locally as 'the great evacuation'. For seven months the people of the area round Slapton, Strete and Stokenham were turned out of their homes, while the American army trained for Normandy. (There had been some successful manœuvres in the same place in 1938, when a rising commander called Montgomery led the invading force, so perhaps he remembered.) It was widely said at the time that this would mean the end of life in these villages, for nobody would go back; but back they went. The Americans, to mark their appreciation, left a fine obelisk at Slapton on the 'line' – a bar of land stretching between a fresh water lake and the sea. A good deal of damage was done, inevitably. Stokenham church was knocked about. The Royal Sands Hotel, a famous fishing inn on the line, was made rubble. A few years later I was travelling past there by bus, and two visitors, clearly transatlantic, noticing the ruin, ascribed it to the Germans with suitable commiserations. An old countrywoman, about to leave the bus, shook her head at them.

''Tweren't the Germans, m'dears,' she said severely. (Of course she knew where they came from.) ''Twas the Americans.'

'The Americans?'

'Ais. They dratted Americans. 'Twas they as did the bombing o' we.'

She departed in a pregnant and baffled silence. Nobody else on the bus saw fit to enlighten the guests. But the hard feelings did not last long. (I should add that their informant was doing the Americans an injustice, since an accidentally-exploded land mine, in 1940, did most of the damage to the hotel.)

In 1944 father moved from Falmouth to Totnes, the pretty, ancient country town which is the northern gateway of the South Hams. I went on living in Totnes after my marriage in 1948, so I was placed conveniently for my work. The Manse at Totnes was quite the nicest we ever had, looking across the Dart at the old town on its steep little hill. The church was smaller than the Falmouth one, but at the age of 54 that suited father well enough. The church people were friendly and intelligent. These were, on the whole, good years. When I look back on Totnes I see it in sunshine and not rain or cold, which is a good index to whether you have been happy in a place. I was very busy, lecturing five evenings a week, and perhaps an afternoon or two as well; writing a powerful political tract which I am glad to say never saw the light of day. I was fit enough to play some rugby for the Totnes club, and I was much in demand as a lay preacher, especially in Methodist chapels.

The Baptists, unlike the Methodists, do not depend upon lay preachers to sustain their preaching ministry. The Methodist 'local preacher', as they prefer to call him, is one of the key figures in modern English religious history. The network of Methodist chapels in such areas as the west of England could not be kept supplied with preachers were it not for the 'locals'. Whatever may once have been the case, they are not semi-literate. They need to pass examinations to qualify for the work. It is true that many of them are craftsmen rather than architects, better at the routine of sermon-making than the grand design of theology. But so far as the technique of preaching goes, many Methodist local preachers could give points and a beating to many Anglican parsons.

A remarkable and not sufficiently known book, by Beatrice Hawker, called *Look Back in Love*,[1] contains many reminiscences of the life of a Methodist local preacher in the west of England. It inadvertently illustrates the point I have just made: because it becomes increasingly clear that Mrs Hawker, obviously a highly effective preacher in the technical sense, never had any clear idea of what she was preaching *about*. In the end she is drawn to Roman Catholicism, seeking precisely those attributes of authority and grandeur which the Wesleys provide in abundance, of which she had so often spoken and sung – but which she had never comprehended. I do not know that I blame her too much. There is so much of blinding light in the Wesleys, especially in the hymns of Charles, that it is easier not to look at it.

A Baptist lay preacher has fewer advantages than a Methodist local preacher. He is confessedly a substitute, someone to be put up with, lacking the magic Reverend. He does not need to pass any examinations; it is up to the church concerned to invite him. On the other hand, he usually gets paid, which Methodist local preachers do not. On the occasions when I was asked to preach in Methodist churches I caused something of a furore by stipulating (if the church was of any size) a

1. Longmans, Green, 1958.

fee of one guinea. I did not usually keep it for myself, but there was no reason why I should not have done. In Baptist or Congregational churches the labourer is considered worthy of his hire.

To begin with, I was very much a pulpit-thumping preacher, with perorations full of *hwyl*. This style was all very well in a big church with a big congregation, but naturally I was not very often asked to preach in such places. It was an unsuitable style for a dozen dozy Devonians in a village chapel on a warm Sunday afternoon; or half a dozen chilly Cornishmen in a vast barn of a building on a cold winter evening. O, those Cornish Methodist chapels! Sometimes there were two or three of them in one tiny village, each big enough to seat the entire population twice over. Many of them were built for nineteenth-century revivals. The Primitive Methodists would have a revival, then the Methodist New Connexion would have a revival, then the Bible Christians would have a revival – and every revival left a new, large, empty church behind it. When Methodist union came in the early thirties, it was only nominal in many parts of Cornwall. During the war the Wesley church at Falmouth was bombed, and its congregation was given refuge in Berkeley Vale church, about a hundred yards away. Berkeley Vale, while Methodist, was not Wesleyan. Although the two congregations worshipped together, each occupied its own side of the church, to discourage unnecessary fraternization. It reminded me of Exeter cathedral during the Interregnum, when a wall was built between the nave and the chancel so that Presbyterians could worship in one part, Independents in the other.

I enjoyed, and I valued, my preaching experience, and still add to it from time to time. Apart from anything else, the Dissenting chapels of the west provide an incomparable training in public speaking. To hold the attention of that assortment of congregations in those assorted circumstances was much more difficult than speaking at the Oxford Union. I soon found I had to abandon most of the rhetoric: but even so the congregations required a sermon – not, the pop word of another generation, an 'address'. They demanded a good grounding in the Bible. They knew the Bible, and expected the preacher to know it. They liked an exordium, a firstly, a secondly, a thirdly, and a finally. The anecdotal style, which I have often heard from Anglican clergy (story+moral=ten minutes) would not do at all for the Methodists of Carnmenellis. Twenty minutes is par for the course, even today.

The words *church* and *chapel*, incidentally, are interchangeable in Dissenting use. It is true that we speak, sometimes, of a building as the *chapel* rather than the *church*, and that we speak of a 'church meeting' rather than a 'chapel meeting'. This is because a church consists of people, and a chapel of stones, and it is sensible to keep the more important word for the more important thing. But the division of church/chapel in the sense Anglican/Nonconformist is invalid. I suspect it became current through supercilious Anglicans and aggressive Nonconformists, both anxious to emphasize their differences.

Another terminological point: I have sometimes used this word 'Nonconformists', because it is a convenient word to include Methodists. Methodists are not, and do not often like being called, Dissenters. Dissenters is the hallowed name of those who broke away from the Church of England in the sixteenth and seventeenth centuries, chiefly because of the notion of the 'gathered church', the New Testament church as they believed. The Methodists left for different reasons in a different age. Baptists, Congregationalists, Presbyterians (in England) and sundry other descendants of the seventeenth-century sects – these are the people for whom the word

'Dissenters' should be used. 'Nonconformists' is a colourless word, though I suppose better than the priggish 'Free Churchmen'. Soon, all being well, the Methodists will have returned to the Anglicans, or *vice versa*, and we can go back to 'Dissenters' for the rest of us.

Soon, indeed, I hope there need be no more Dissenters, in the sense of separate denominations. But so much has been written about the question of Christian unity that I shall not seek to enlarge upon it: except to recount one incident which occurred in my own experience. For about a year of my life I was preoccupied with this particular problem. I prayed about it more regularly, and more earnestly, than I have ever prayed about anything else. When things looked as if they were going wrong, I embarked on a personal twenty-four-hour fast, not telling anybody. How much it seemed to matter! It is some comfort, twenty years afterwards, to feel that it did matter. At least, ideas which were then pioneering are now commonplace, ecumenically, and this is one indication of progress. I do not believe in 'progress' in the sense of any gradual or lasting improvement of the human condition, but this does not mean I share the full Calvinist doctrine of total depravity. It is possible to improve in some ways, and necessary to do so to balance other ways in which we decline. Thus every generation has different merits and different faults, but it would only be the generation that stopped trying which could be called totally corrupt.

After this fine talk the incident itself seems trivial enough. The Baptist and Congregational churches at Totnes were built close together, and neither was specially well attended. Soon after the war the Congregational minister moved on, and the question arose whether it might not be better to have one church (and one chapel) rather than two. I do not remember who first thought of this idea, but the two men who did most to carry it through, after great difficulties, were Fred Todkill and my father.

Fred Todkill was a Yorkshireman, who had come down to Devon as manager of the textile mill at Dartington (the prettiest textile mill in the country, water-wheel and all, and it still makes superb cloth). I use the past tense about Fred only because I have lost touch with him. He was a remarkable man. He might have been a professional singer, or even a professional cricketer, had he chosen those paths. He was the secretary of the Congregational church in Totnes. As a practical Yorkshireman, he saw the economic advantage of union between the two churches. But – also as a practical Yorkshireman – he was heart and soul with the ecumenical movement (a clumsy phrase for which we still have to find a better). The divisions of the church were, to him, nonsense. In this he was representative of the best type of Christian in every denomination down the ages – the humble, straightforward man, layman or ordained, who keeps the Church going – for all the bishops and moderators can do. As Jowett said to Margot Asquith, 'My dear child, you must believe in God in spite of what the clergy tell you.'[1]

Father was a more complicated case. In his early days in the ministry he liked to call himself a 'hard-boiled Baptist'. He was sensitive about his lack of formal education, and rankled at any Anglican slurs. When I was to be married, it was naturally thought that the best place for it would be the parish church of Dursley, where my prospective wife lived, and where her family attended. But could my father, we wondered, take some part in the service? Yes, he could: he could give an address – provided that he did so (a) after the benediction had

1. *The Autobiography of Margot Asquith*. Penguin Books, 1936, vol. 1, p. 117. Jowett was not just being cynical: he had just recovered from a serious illness and was answering a question about his reactions to it.

been pronounced, and (b) from the chancel steps, or some other appropriate place, but *not* the pulpit. He wrote to the Vicar, who had laid down these instructions, and said he felt they were 'an insult to his orders'. Later in my life it happened that I preached, Baptist layman that I was, in three Anglican cathedrals. I made sure that I preached from the pulpit, before the benediction. I confess to an un-Christian, un-ecumenical feeling that I squared that particular account.

The incident shows how fraught with danger relations between Anglicans and Dissenters could be, even so recently. It also shows that even by that time my father still possessed a proper sense of denominational pride. His idea of church unity was that the others should see the light and become Baptists. But he was a man of compassion, of a generous spirit, and in Totnes he was confronted with a situation where, if he modified his views (but there were some who would say 'threw away his principles') he could achieve a more immediate and practical good than if he stuck to them. Later he came to believe that unity was much more than this. He read Temple on St John, and kept recurring to the seventeenth chapter: '*that they all may be one . . . that the world may believe that thou hast sent me . . . that they may be one, even as we are one.*' Temple wrote: 'The unity which the Lord prays that his disciples may enjoy is that which is eternally characteristic of the Triune God. It is, therefore, something much more than a means to any end – even though that end be the evangelization of the world; it is itself the one worthy end of all human aspiration; it is the life of heaven.'[1] Father came to believe this and to communicate it. But I think he was first attracted to the idea of unity with the Congregational Church simply because he wanted to get the visiting of the sick better organized, and the young people together in works of practical

1. William Temple. *Readings in St John's Gospel*. Macmillan, 1949, p. 320.

goodwill. Anyway, sometimes kicking but never screaming, he was drawn into the ecumenical movement, and the Baptist and Congregational churches of Totnes became, and remain, under the blessing of God, the Totnes United Free Church.

The particular difficulties that attended the operation are not worth rehearsing. What did strike me, however, and has often struck me since in similar operations which I have encountered, was that the hardest problems were not doctrinal. The questions were not, 'How can we reconcile our views on baptism?' or 'How are we to define church membership?' They were, 'Which building shall we use?' and 'What's going to happen to the rent of those cottages out at Harbertonford?' It is not theology that really stands in the way of Christian unity.

Let me set down one or two more things about my father. His taste in poetry, for instance: it would certainly be called today (and was called then, by me) execrable. He had been known to end a sermon with 'Mother of Mine', and on the great reunion day was tempted to finish with 'Pioneers! O pioneers!' He was fond of Campbell, and anything which could be chanted aloud, and as he was going about his business would suddenly burst out into such snatches as,

> 'Now who be ye, would cross Lochgyle
>   This dark and stormy water?'
> 'O, I'm the chief of Ulva's isle,
>   And this, Lord Ullin's daughter!'

I inherited this trait, and I am bound to say it has given me much delight, though my family has sometimes found it trying.

He had a beautifully pure, though of course quite untrained tenor voice, and was much in demand at church socials for 'I'll Walk Beside You', 'Silent Worship', and (always the encore) 'Passing By'. He had an instinct for music, and although he could not read it had picked up enough to accompany a service on the piano or harmonium. He loved the organ, and was anxious that I should become proficient at it, but despite years of hardly-afforded lessons I disappointed him.

Father always thought the best of people, though no fool. He was often imposed upon, but he maintained it was better to be imposed upon than to miss a chance of helping someone. He believed that the only things we possess are those we give away. He lived, as Virgil says the Emperor Titus did, as though the day was lost on which he did no good thing.

His health was always poor after he was gassed in the war. This so affected his sight that at one time it was thought he would go blind. For a while he quietly practised walking about with his eyes closed, to get used to it. This, however, he was spared. He died in 1950, of cancer, but with little pain. He was fifty-nine years old. I have always missed him, but never mourned him.

> No, dear companion, no:
> We gladly let thee go
> From a suffering church beneath
> To a reigning church above:
> Thou hast more than conquered death
> Thou art crowned with life and love.

I placed these words, with my wreath, upon my father's grave. His funeral was private, but we had a crowded service of thanksgiving in the United Free Church, and we sang, 'How sweet the Name of Jesus sounds', and 'In heavenly love abiding', and 'There is a land of pure delight', than which there can be no better hymns for the farewell to a father of the Dissenting people. I look back on the service itself with entire happiness. Mother could not quite bring herself to go to the service, but bravely did not go into mourning, which he would not have liked. Coveys of father's relations from the north descended in their best blacks, and I was not very popular with one or two of them, because we had decided there would be no 'family oop froont', and did not provide Pharaoh's basket of bakemeats. But they were friendly, jolly people, and though most of them were to be separated from me by distance, age and taste, I have never altogether lost touch with them. I like to think I am the grandson of that formidable old Mrs Gibson who set up the lemonade stall at the Durham Gala.

I am glad to think that when father died my own barometer seemed set fair. I was married, we had a little boy, and I had a good job with an organization which at that time seemed to combine the qualities of glamour and righteousness: the BBC.

7 Plymouth

In 1948 I wrote to Frank Gillard, then Head of West Regional Programmes (HWRP, in the jargon beloved of the BBC) and suggested myself as a broadcaster. I remember specifying the fields of cricket commentary and poetry reading.

I was happy in my job at the University, but it was poorly paid for a family man. In the first place I thought of broadcasting simply as a chance of earning some supplementary money.

The first broadcast I made was when I read a short story (not my own) in a series from Bristol entitled 'Stories from Studio Five'. Studio Five, Bristol, stands today much as it did then – a relic of the original house which the BBC had taken over: ornate, pillared, and with a shocking acoustic. It reminds me a little of the porch of St Mary's, Oxford. It also reminds me of the remark of Vaughan Williams, concerning the harpsichord: 'O 'ow I 'ate all that baroque buggery.'[1]

I was announced by Keith Hamilton Price, who was to be a friend for many years. Our conversation, immediately prior to going on the air, was as follows:

K.H.P.: Done much of this before?
A.G. (palpitating): Er, no.
K.H.P. (radiating assurance): There's nothing to it.

1. It must not be thought from this anecdote that V.W. habitually dropped his aitches. He was clearly echoing the remark made about a learned judge in the Law Courts, *circa* 1880: ' 'Ere 'e comes, the 'oly 'umbug, 'umming 'is 'ymn. 'Ow I 'ate 'im!' (Geoffrey Dearmer, *Songs of Praise Discussed*, OUP, 1933, p. 123, cites the original.) I have, however, the evidence of Kenneth Savidge, who was present, that V.W. was absent-mindedly putting his fork into his ear as he made this observation.

I discovered later that he was in his first week as an announcer, and about as scared as I was.

My producer was Gilbert Phelps. He was the old style of talks producer, who would work through a script sentence by sentence. That was the great period of the fifteen-minute talk or story. Today the emphasis is on the three-minuter, or less; capsule broadcasting; and such meticulous preparation is thought unnecessary, which is why we hear so many broadcasts where it sounds as though script and speaker were making each other's acquaintance for the first time.

My second broadcast was a short account for 'Sport in the West' of the cricket between the Australians and Somerset, at Taunton. That same day I had an audition as a cricket commentator, i.e. a 'running commentator' (a horrible phrase, but I suppose we are lumbered with it now). John Arlott was broadcasting the genuine commentary on this match, and when it was time for my audition he tactfully asked whether I would prefer him to stay in the box or go away for a while. This was a typically thoughtful gesture from a man who has always been kindness itself to me. But there was more to it than met the eye. Even in those days, the amount of cricket commentary broadcast by the BBC was limited, and the arrival of a new commentator, however thin a slice of the cake he might be likely to get, meant that little less for the established feeders. Certainly I did not envisage myself rivalling the incomparable John, nor have I ever done so: but we were, theoretically, competitors in the same field. Yet after the audition he spent a long time offering his ideas on how best to set about the job. I wish I could say that in later years, having become established after a fashion myself, I had always been so generous to younger men.

In the next year I broadcast in various capacities perhaps a couple of dozen times, and then there came a letter from

Frank Gillard drawing my attention to a forthcoming vacancy on the staff of the BBC at Plymouth. 'It would be improper for me to say more,' he punctiliously added.

My wife and I were still living at Totnes, less than twenty-five miles away, so it would be possible to work in Plymouth without moving house – an important consideration in those days of desperate housing shortage. I was, however, not at all sure that I wanted the job. I had long assumed, without thinking about it much, that one way or another I would have an academic career. The post at Plymouth was essentially that of a news reporter. I had little experience of news reporting, and was not attracted to it. On the other hand, there was some magic, then, about being 'something at the BBC'.

I discovered, however, that the BBC did not really want me as a news reporter. The post for which I was applying was going to be abolished. Instead, a 'General Programme Assistant' was to be appointed, with wider responsibilities and a higher salary. This latter post, for complicated internal reasons, would only be open to staff applicants. It was therefore necessary for me to apply for a job which I did not much care for, and which was doomed, in order to become a designate member of the staff, and thus enabled to apply for another. So I applied, the procedure was solemnly gone through, and – not altogether to my surprise – I became, initials and all, GPA, Plymouth.

In terms of my working life this was the most important decision I have ever taken. Other important decisions came later, but this was the governing one. Looking back from the age of fifty-two I think it was a mistake, and that I would have had a happier life if I had kept broadcasting as a spare-time interest; but that is a view blessed by hindsight. An academic base, with only occasional forays beyond it, seems now to me a much more civilized way of living: but we all know on which side of the fence the grass is greener.

The BBC at Plymouth was a small, pleasant station. The total staff was perhaps twenty-five. There were three producers: Brandon Acton-Bond (drama), Mollie Austin (Children's Hour) and me. General Programme Assistant was not as impressive as it sounds – I was really the station's odd-job man – but the work was varied and gave me a thorough grounding in sound broadcasting. I travelled the west country constantly, which was delightful, and there were always interesting people to be met.

One or two of the programmes I did in those days stay in my memory. There was a series called 'Village on the Air'. I would spend perhaps three days in a village, and would be joined on the last day by a recording engineer. I would then edit the recordings of the inhabitants in the studio, and link them, seeking to present in fifteen minutes a picture of the village and its life. The editing was a much more formidable task than it would be today. It was before the days of tape recording, and editing discs was hard work. Furthermore, the recording cars, though big Humber Pullmans (*how* we swaggered with them, we young men) could only carry one machine, so the duration of each recording was limited to about four minutes, after which there would be a break while the engineer changed discs. This meant either interrupting the person one was talking to, and possibly putting him out of his stride, or carrying hopefully on, in which case the best bits always occurred while the change-overs were taking place.

They were lovely days, in those villages: Steeple Ashton, Briantspuddle, Sixpenny Handley (villages with attractive names stood a better chance of being chosen). Sometimes the weather was harsh, for we recorded the programme in winter. One cold night at Hartland, on the tip of north Devon, I was the only guest in a large, freezing hotel. I arrived in the dark, and when I awoke in the morning there was the Atlantic outside the window – and I had the lines to greet it, for they had been among father's favourites –

> '. . . where on Hartland's tempest-furrowed shore
> Breaks the long swell from farthest Labrador'

– though why *farthest* Labrador I am not sure; nor even who wrote them; nor even whether I have got them right. Still, it was a poetic experience to proclaim them as the spray came across the windows. That most of the poetic experiences I can recall have been associated with verse of possibly poor and certainly unfashionable quality demonstrates not that the experience was false, but merely that my character falls short of the sublime.

Even then the increase in mass communications was making village life more standardized, but I do not share the view that either village character or village 'characters' have disappeared, though no doubt they take longer to discover. Bernard Fishwick, a shrewd and genial man, and one of the best broadcasters to come out of the west, told me – when I took over 'Village on the Air' from him (this was no slight on Bernard: he had been called to higher things) – 'Start with the parson and the pub.' Parsons and pubs are two aspects of village life which have mostly retained their character. Pubs have influenced my life as much as parsons. Only by stern self-control do I prevent myself from breaking into a litany of my favourite pubs: that, and the fact that there would always be one more which did not deserve to be left out. I compiled some programmes about pubs, called (it was not my title) 'Inns and Outs'. The research was strenuous. The earliest recordings of the day were crisp and businesslike, but by the time we had reached our evening ports of call my interviewing was not incisive. The recording engineer, fortunately, was a teetotaller.

I had never drunk beer until I was at Oxford. Indeed, my parents were under the impression that I was teetotal for some time after that, until I arrived home late one night roaring drunk after a Totnes rugby dinner (I think it is fair to say that the lads intended me to go home drunk that night). After the usual preliminary distaste I took to beer like a brother, and a good friendly brother it has always been. There have been times when I have abused it, but that was my fault, not beer's. I respect wine, but have not really the palate nor the patience for it. Spirits are treacherous, even good whisky. Ale, if not so brisk a pipe as poetry, is the stuff to drink.

When I first worked at Plymouth it was a little short of good pubs, partly as a result of the wartime bombing. Things are better now. Although during the war other cities suffered a heavier load of bombs than Plymouth, nowhere was the bombing more concentrated. Since the city is on a kind of peninsula between the river Tamar and the river Plym, and since any part of it could then reasonably be called a military objective, the bombers only had to line up the two rivers and drop their bombs in between. This meant that only a few buildings were left standing in the town's centre, and gave a unique opportunity of planning again from scratch. Pre-war Plymouth had been a frantic tangle of traffic and narrow streets. Courageously, the city fathers began by knocking down what was left – apart from a few distinguished buildings which could be fitted into the new plan. The result is a city centre as nearly pleasant as such a place can be. It still lacks what is called 'character', but what gives a city character are the bits of nonsense that grow up over centuries, and nobody can sit down and invent suitable bits of nonsense for the purpose. They will grow. In some areas, such as the Barbican down by Sutton Pool, they have never been destroyed.

The Barbican brings me to Isaac Foot, who was born there, and his remarkable family. What with broadcasting and politics, I came to know them quite well, especially John. Of the five sons, Dingle served in the ministry of Sir Winston Churchill during the war, and should have been leader of the Liberal party after it; but he lost his seat in Dundee, a big, awkward, double-member constituency; fought North Cornwall, which we had held at the previous election, and lost that too; joined the Labour party and became Solicitor-General under Harold Wilson. He does not seem to have been exceptionally successful or exceptionally happy in the Labour party. I was very bitter when he left us, which was not very sensible of me, since a man is entitled to change his party whenever he likes, an obvious enough proposition when you come to think of it. Still, we had been having a desperate struggle to keep the Liberals going, and his departure, the circumstances of which were not altogether fortunate, was a heavy blow.

Hugh Foot, the second son, now Lord Caradon, I have met only occasionally. He was too busy travelling the world, setting Nigeria or Cyprus or the United Nations to rights, to be in Plymouth much: a very considerable man, with more of his father in him, I should guess, than any of the others. Michael, who is the fourth son, is the charmer of the family. He represented Devonport for Labour when J. J. Astor represented Sutton (the other Plymouth division) for the Conservatives, and I once heard J. J. Astor say, 'I like Michael so much because he's the only member of the family who doesn't think God is a Foot.' Christopher, the fifth son, was a genial and witty companion. He has not suffered from being the youngest boy of so formidable a brood. He has, perhaps, suffered a little from hearing people suggest it.

That leaves John, faithful Liberal John, shrewd and sardonic John, a man of the warmest heart who spends much time trying to conceal it. John ran the family business in Plymouth and is now, Curzon bless us, Lord Foot. (When he was given his life peerage brother Dingle observed that it was enough to make the blood run blue.) I refrain from saying more about John, in recent years my colleague in 'Round Britain Quiz', because I have said enough already to endanger a long and valued friendship.

All five sons and the father met together – it was the first time for many years – in a BBC studio at Plymouth, in 1952. Their conversation was recorded, and an edited version of it broadcast shortly afterwards. It was one of the best programmes with which I have been associated, though it would have been better had I been a more experienced producer, and had we then been more accustomed to the possibilities of tape recording. Their voices, while recognisable separately, were so much of the same timbre when put together that it was often hard to remember who was who: except, of course, for the great old man. He ended the programme by saying, 'When I got married I had seven different theories about bringing up children. Now I have seven children [there are two daughters] and no theories at all.' As he had two sons in the Commons and two in the Lords, he did not do so badly. His family has not, for the most part, shared his devout Methodism, nor his views on temperance, nor even his belief in the importance of the Liberal party. But he thought the world of them, and so did they of him. It was moving to see them together.

The two men I have met, other than casually, who had the noblest air about them, were Isaac Foot and C. B. Fry. Foot was the greater man, I think, for besides his pride of bearing, and assurance of probity, he had an inner humility which I doubt if Fry quite achieved. Oliver Cromwell wrote to the Scottish ministers – whom he did not want to fight – 'I beseech you, in the bowels of Christ, *think it possible you may be mistaken*.' Isaac Foot might accept so simply modest an appeal. C. B. Fry would be more inclined to sweep it aside, to drown it in the flood of his eloquence. Fry had spoken, what more to be said? Yet when F. E. Smith, visiting Fry on his ship *Mercury*, where he was training young men for the sea, said, 'This is a fine show, C.B., but for you a backwater' – then Fry replied: 'That may be, but the question remains whether it is better to be successful . . . or happy.' Those are words which Isaac Foot would have echoed. Neither man could be called unsuccessful: but both would have cut bigger figures in the world had they been less fastidious about what seemed to them not only right, but proper, and good: or, to use an analogy which I think neither would resent, had they bowed the knee in the house of Rimmon.

It was a pity Isaac Foot did not write more. We have a surfeit of political memoirs, but we could still have done with his. He was a voracious reader, and his house was so full of books that they were liable to spill out of the windows. He had great enthusiasms: Cromwell, Wesley, Napoleon, Wordsworth, and for a while Hazlitt, the one which possibly meant most to his sons. When he had seized on a subject he would not rest until he had read everything about it on which he could lay his hands. You could not talk to him for five minutes without learning something, usually something surprising. His knowledge of the West Country was deep. Dingle in a happy phrase called him 'a kind of West Country John Burns'. It was John Burns who had written of the Thames as 'liquid history', and all the shores and estuaries of the south-west were liquid history to Isaac Foot.

He was also a striking example of those mirthful Puritans of whom I have written earlier. Despite the strictness of his views he was full of humour. When the family were living at St Cleer, near Bodmin, they owned a donkey, and Isaac Foot received a letter from the local authority, informing him that protests had been made about the depredations of this donkey upon neighbouring property. He replied, 'For myself, I am powerless to control the animal, but I have read your letter to the donkey . . .' He was a splendid broadcaster, though a holy terror to his producers, because of his refusal to work to a script, or to run to time. He once delayed the Sunday evening serial because he overran his time on 'The Week's Good Cause'. This was an achievement you would have hardly, in those days, believed possible. Nobody dared to fade him out, certainly not I, the wretched producer. On these occasions he would apologize afterwards, with an impish innocence which was entirely disarming.

When he died there was a memorial service to him in the Central Hall, Plymouth, and all the pride of the city was there. We had a hymn which had been one of his favourites, which had been lately upon his lips. It is Charles Wesley at his most daring and sublime, when he takes the tenderest images of the passion, and sets them to a dance rhythm: joy and solemnity mingling.

> Ah! shew me that happiest place,
>   The place of thy people's abode,
> Where saints in an ecstasy gaze
>   And hang on a crucified God:
>
> 'Tis there I would always abide,
>   And never a moment depart,
> Concealed in the cleft of thy side,
>   Eternally held in thy heart.

Nothing was there for tears.

8 Sparkwell

Sparkwell is a village about eight miles out from Plymouth, near Cornwood, in the foothills of Dartmoor. It is not an especially beautiful village. It consists mostly of a small housing estate, built in the '30s. We lived there for some years. We had a wing of a large country house, built in the nineteenth century, which had once belonged to Charlotte M. Yonge. The bell-indicator in the kitchen was inscribed with the legends, 'Miss Yonge's Bedroom', 'Miss Yonge's Boudoir'. We paid an absurdly high rent, but by vacating our flat in Totnes we made a space for my widowed mother, and the distance to the office in Plymouth was much less. My mother lived in Totnes for the remaining years of her life, somewhat cheerlessly but in less actual discomfort than most widows of Baptist ministers suffer. Whether we ought to have asked her to live with us was a subject upon which she and my wife held differing views. I think that everyone was less unhappy, including mother, by her staying in Totnes. I cannot be sure about this. But her visits almost always ended in disaster. She felt we were living wickedly. Certainly I drank beer, my wife used lipstick, we took Sunday papers, we played pop records, we did not attend church regularly, we did not eat four meals a day at specific times. Mother was sincerely grieved by all this, and wished to save us from our follies. It was probably better that she stayed away.

Olwen, my first wife, was a girl of exceptional beauty and intelligence, whom I met at Oxford. Neither of us had had lovers before, in any serious sense. This was, by Dissenting or even Anglican standards (Olwen came from a Church of

England family) correct, though I have never recommended my children to be so abstemious. We ought to have made a good marriage. All our friends and relations cheered us confidently on. We had some good times together, and we produced two sons of whom we are both proud. But we did not turn out to be well matched: we argued too often, each accustomed to taking the lead in the conversation, and we married too soon, too innocently, before we were ready for it. At this time in our lives my mother was an extra element of tension.

The nature of my work did not assist a happy marriage. Broadcasting then was for me an endless hurdle race, with the distance between the hurdles varying so much that you could not take them rhythmically. As my career grew, so did the amount of nervous energy I consumed. There was a period when I wondered whether I was going to be sick before the broadcast, or, much worse, after it.

Yet I enjoyed my work. Few people could have failed to enjoy a job with such variety. I wrote and produced, for instance, a series called 'A Page of History', dramatized versions of great occasions in the history of the west. A good deal of research went into this series, although when I look today at such scripts as have survived, I find the treatment and dialogue raw, to put it kindly. For a season, I produced 'At the Luscombes', which could be described as the West Region's soap opera were it not that the scripts of Denis Constanduros raised it to a level much higher than most such programmes achieve. For a while I was producer of 'The Archaeologist', which extended my knowledge, and brought some pleasant visits to digs around the country in the company of Glyn Daniel, who introduced the programme. I was producer of 'Speak Your Mind!' a programme in which members of the public gave their own views on questions of the day: a good programme at its best, though often depressing. We toured, mostly, the country towns – places then thought to be too small for 'Any Questions?' and too big for 'Village on the Air'. They were pleasant places to visit, but the audiences were usually heavily conservative, and horsewhips were mentioned more than once. The chairman of this programme at that time was Gordon McMurtrie, a brisk, breezy character who became Recorder of Newton Abbot. He had met Frank Gillard during the war, and Frank had been sure that McMurtrie would make a strong broadcasting personality. I did not know McMurtrie, but had conceived an aversion to him on the air. I had no idea, when summoned to Frank's presence one day, that I was likely to be involved with him. After talking about other things than the one he meant to talk about – as was his wont – Frank said:

'By the way, what do you think of Gordon McMurtrie as a broadcaster?'

A.G. (casually): I think he stinks.

F.G. Oh . . . well, in that case, it seems to me you're the ideal person to produce him.

Despite this inauspicious beginning, I found that Frank's estimate was right, and McMurtrie and I did some capital programmes together. Certainly he was a terrible Tory, but he manfully tried to remain impartial (though once, on the question of flogging, he inadvertently slipped into the position of cheer-leader). He had a quick, robust wit, and was good company.

Then there was a long and arduous programme about Dartington Hall, in which I was assistant producer to Robert Waller, but the principal genius of which was Victor Bonham Carter. It was as a result of this programme that he wrote his excellent history of the new Dartington. I must say a little about Dartington because, for so long as I lived in Devon, and especially when I lived in Totnes, less than a couple of miles away, it was a big influence in my life. For one thing, the Dartington summer music festivals were something one could not normally expect to find in the countryside.

Dartington Hall, the ancestral home of the Champernowne family, was bought by Mr and Mrs L. K. Elmhirst in 1926. Dorothy Elmhirst had been left a large sum of money to be used for educational purposes, and she and her husband chose Dartington as the site for what they called 'an experiment in rural reconstruction'. They took over a ruined tower, a tumbledown hall, an overrun quadrangle – but some good land. That was the time when everyone was mourning 'the drift from the countryside'. The Elmhirsts recognized that bird song, and the wind in the trees, are not for most people a sufficient substitute for running water and electric light, educational opportunity and social activity. They set out to create a rural estate which combined civic amenity with country beauty – that puts it clumsily, but Dartington is hardly to be summed in a phrase. The word most commonly used about it, by those who did not know it, was 'aery-faery'. But the Elmhirsts were practical people. If one of their local industries failed, they closed it; they did not take the easy way out, and put in a bit more capital – not when the industry had had a fair trial. They had a dairy farm, a sawmill, a textile mill (of which Fred Todkill was manager), all of which paid their way. There was an arts department, an adult education department, and a school. The school was one of the first of the kind we now call 'progressive'. In some ways it was certainly ahead of its time. Totnes people were often startled by the hair styles, the orange jackets and purple slacks, the assured demeanour of Dartington children whom they encountered shopping in that venerable Fore Street. The school has had its difficulties since, but it was undoubtedly a success under W. B. Curry. But then Curry was an outstanding headmaster, who would have made any system work well.

I suppose the social ideas of the whole Dartington experiment are now considered *vieux jeux*. Yet there was a fine, challenging spirit there, and many minds at once conscientious and bold. From those friends, and colleagues in assorted enterprises, I now particularly recall one, a master at the school, who died perhaps ten years ago.

His name was Federico de La Iglesia. He was a Spaniard. He commanded an army in the last days of Madrid. I remember him for many things, but especially because he saw Devon with different eyes from the rest of us. He would point out what is – when you come to think of it – a baffling contradiction in Devon history. For this was the land, as he had learnt in his childhood, of the dark and harsh and terrible men, of the merciless Protestants. This was the county of the heathen buccaneers, of El Draque, who had destroyed the crusaders of Philip. Devon was the country of beetling cliffs and beetling brows, of barbarian voices crying,

Ho! We revel in our chains, for the sorrow that was Spain's!

And when he came to Devon to live, rather reluctantly and anxiously, Federico could not understand the contrast: this gentle countryside, these mild people, slow-spoken, brows never beetling save on a poor crop or a muddy pint of cider. 'I thought it was all a bluff,' he used to say. 'Whenever I saw a cow peering over a hedge [the big South Devon cows, the orange elephants] that cow was saying, "We're watching you, you dirty Spaniard, you and your bullfights, just you wait!" ' Federico was a friend to treasure: shiny hair, dark little moustache, a command of English good enough to enable him to earn a living teaching English history in English, at a glance you might have taken him for the traditional English caricature of a Spaniard – but only at a glance. His approach to life was both detached and warm, and he was as good a Liberal as Isaac Foot. His view of the communists was that they were the best allies so long as things were difficult: 'but if we had won I dare say I should have had to run for it, just as I had to do when we lost.' He had no illusions, but still contrived to love his fellow men. His was the Catholic mind at its best, and as I was still inclined to be a bigoted Protestant his friendship did me much good.

Not all the Devon countryside is gentle. Go only a few miles north from Dartington and you reach Dartmoor, much more in accordance with the Devon Federico had imagined. The moor has grandeur rather than beauty. It is often bleak. The prison at Princetown emphasizes the bleakness. I knew it quite well at one time, as a visiting lecturer, and also because of some broadcasting.

The chaplain at Dartmoor then was Leslie Lloyd Rees, and he gave a striking half-hour broadcast about his work, illustrated by recordings which we had made inside the prison. He had great enthusiasm for his work. He liked the men (more difficult than loving them, perhaps), and clearly they liked him. If there were men he found it difficult to like he tried to act as though he did (a good tip for all unsuccessful Christians). *The moor* is where the recidivists go, and so he knew that he would have many disappointments: if as many as 45 per cent did not return to prison he was doing well – 'and I dare say most of those,' he would say, 'don't come back because they haven't been caught, or are dead.' He found it a valuable discipline to seek to do good, *without* expectation of reward.

Lloyd Rees had been a useful amateur boxer, and when Freddie Mills visited the prison they boxed three rounds. It was fun to hear him reading out the football results. The cheers and groans from the different localities, in accents distinguishable even *en masse*, resounded round the hall. Since he was Welsh, special attention was always paid to Cardiff City. But he was much more than a library-and-concert chaplain. He had a cure of souls. The Christian religion is meant for sinners, so prison is a good place to preach it. During his broadcast we heard the men singing at their communion service,

> Look, Father, look on His anointed face,
>   And only look on us as seen in Him;
> Look not on our misusings of thy grace,
>   Our prayer so languid, and our faith so dim:
> For, lo! between our sins and their reward
>   We set the passion of thy son, our Lord.

'What can be more relevant than that?' asked Lloyd Rees.

It was the success of this broadcast which gave Martin Willson, the director of religious programmes for the West Region, the idea of broadcasting a 'Sunday Half Hour' of hymn-singing from the prison. This duly took place, and though there were some protests most people found it moving. There had been a good deal of preliminary argument with the Home Office. They were quite prepared to approve of the programme – provided it was pre-recorded. But 'Sunday Half Hour' was then never pre-recorded, and to change the custom in this case would have been equivalent to saying we could not trust the men, which would have been equivalent to saying we ought not to be doing the broadcast at all. Pre-recording would in fact have been the likeliest way of getting ourselves into trouble, because the men would have resented the affront. For though it might seem strange to outsiders that such a broadcast should come from such a place, why should those inside find it so? Had they not been told, often enough, that the Christian religion is for sinners? In the end, the Home Office gave way. The broadcast passed off perfectly smoothly. Martin Willson had not sought any special publicity for the programme – the billing appeared in the *Radio Times* in the normal way. This was some years before, with a fanfare of trumpets, a broadcast from Strangeways was announced as the first to be made from a gaol.

Many broadcasts in which I was involved were routine: news and sports reports. I was never much good at hard news, but fortunately in those days the BBC did not expect their reporters to use foot-in-the-door tactics. Sometimes I was sent to write a 'colour' piece on a public event, or one of the West Country's numerous folk festivals. Once is enough for most of these things, especially when there were three or four different pieces on the same occasion, each angled slightly differently for three or four different services. In embittered moments I contemplated bringing out a short monograph to be entitled 'My Hundred Best Broadcasts about Helston Furry'. Nineteen-fifty-one (Festival of Britain) and 1953 (Coronation year) were ferocious years for local festivities. Every parish was digging up an ancient ceremony, or inventing a new one. Here a hundredweight pasty was paraded round the green; there a deer was roasted in the square; thither a medieval tourney was restaged. Everywhere there were pageants. I helped to write a pageant for Totnes, and I narrated 'The Pageant of Plymouth Hoe': six chilly nights on the bleak expanse of the Citadel square, and in a dinner jacket. These things had their moments, but when they were over I found myself inclined to agree with Charles Wesley, that

> Not all the gay pageants that breathe
> Can with a dead body compare.

(I suppose the reading 'pagans' for 'pageants', which most

later editors of Wesley have adopted, is correct; but the misreading is too good to be forgotten.)

The people one met were more fun than the occasions one attended: a fine, mixed bag we have in the west. I remember Mr Victor Stephens of Truro. He was a butcher, who in his spare time bred mice. Up till 1938 he had bred rabbits, but then he moved into a council house and there was no room for rabbits, so he took up mice instead. He had always been fond of mice. When he was a boy his father often took him into the stables, and while father was attending to the horses son would make friends with the field-mice. 'All my life,' said Mr Stephens in an unforgettable phrase, 'I have been a bit of an idealist about mice.' At the time I met him, he had achieved a triumph. He had produced a Marten Sable, the first of a new breed. It was the first new breed to be accepted by the National Mouse Club for more than twenty years. A thoroughbred Marten Sable has to be sepia-coloured on top, shading off to a paler colour lower down, white-bellied, with white ticking on the flanks and rump. It took Mr Stephens two and a half years to produce it. That was only a beginning. His intended masterpiece, his ambition, was a Red Fox mouse, never produced though often imagined. He had been working on that for ten years, the experts said it would take him at least another ten, but he thought he could do it sooner than that. He was also anxious to breed a mouse with spots of three different colours. He had managed mice with spots of three different *shades*, but so had others, and he would not be satisfied until the colours were distinctively different.

He was a little lonely in his hobby. Nobody else in Cornwall shared it. The nearest mice exhibitions were in London. The strongholds of the Fancy – delightfully, they adopted the old boxing term – are the midlands and the north. However, he pointed out, 'I can send two mice to a show anywhere in the country for three and sixpence return, plus a shilling entrance fee.' He had between sixty and seventy mice, which cost him about fourteen shillings a week to keep – about a farthing a day each. (This must have been 1955, or thereabouts.) A mouse can live up to two years, but it is below stud work after one: 'the tails do shorten.' One man's world. I hope Mr Stephens has his Red Fox by now.

One woman's world. Miss Joan Rendell was an idealist too. I met her at her home near Launceston: a brisk, lively lady who had travelled the world in pursuit of her passion for matchbox labels. She had a collection of about 74,000. I called her one of the country's leading phillumenists, which she did not like much, for the sound reason that 'phillumenist' is a bastard mixture of Greek and Latin. The alternative 'phillampadist' has been suggested, but on the whole the fraternity prefer the straightforward 'matchbox label collector'.

The first friction match was made in 1820, and *only nine years later*, Miss Rendell emphasized, there is a reference to collecting labels, in a novel published in France. Early specimens will fetch high prices, running into hundreds of pounds. There are sufficient collectors abroad for Miss Rendell to pay her way round the world lecturing to them, but England is the stronghold. She was worried about developments in the United States, because of the growth of the book match. There are booklet collectors, but the aristocracy of the hobby leaves them alone: there are so many different booklets that it is all too easy.

There is an obvious parallel with stamp collecting, a hobby which I pursued enthusiastically into manhood, and would I dare say still, had not an old friend in an inconsiderate moment stolen my collection. Some countries issue special sets of labels for great occasions, but Britain is backward in this field, just as she was for long with commemorative stamps. Such labels are often printed in sheets, for selling to collectors, and are therefore much more valuable if they can be found in 'used' condition, with match box attached.

I still have several copies, given to me by Miss Rendell, of the newsletter of the British Match Box and Booklet Society. Real devotion to matches shines through the pages. There are, for instance, the Literary References, which consist of reproducing any printed reference, however insignificant, to matches. It is recorded how at the time of the Lynmouth disaster a caravan was sent with supplies for the victims, and its stock included matches. End of item. There are greetings to fellow-members – two Czech members have just got married – the exchange offers, the painstaking cataloguing of past issues.

This was a Japanese wartime propaganda label.

> No. 204. Horizontal. A cigar-smoking Churchill and sweating Roosevelt being prodded by Japanese soldier using bayonet.

Miss Rendell wanted to know if it was true that, in the days of 'spot effects' (i.e. not recorded) in radio, the engineers obtained the effect of a burning house by crumpling a match box. I told her that this could be done, and also of the legendary occasion when the boys burnt down a house to get the effect of crumpling a match box. I hope this duly appeared in the Literary References.

My colleagues in the BBC were an engaging lot. In those days West Region always considered itself the cock of the BBC walk, a view shared to a surprising extent elsewhere. Certainly most of the people who were then run-of-the-mill producers at Bristol and Plymouth have since made names for themselves, one way or another. There was no shortage of character: some of it may have been bad character, or unpredictable character. There was more eccentricity than vice. In all my experience of BBC producers I have only found one crook.

In those days at Plymouth the station was thought sufficiently important to warrant a 'Plymouth Representative', a gentleman of near-Controller rank, though perhaps without a superabundance of duties. Plymouth Representative was Colonel R. S. Stafford; grey, moustached, upright, every inch a colonel. In my first conversation with him, he said, 'Of course, I know nothing about broadcasting.' I agitated my mind for a suitable reply (*Oh, but surely? You don't say? Well, who does?*). I did not know then that Colonel Stafford had joined the BBC before the war as its Defence Officer (disguised as a Talks Producer, so as not to offend Hitler: I have my doubts as to the effectiveness of the disguise). He was a lovable person, and he knew much more about broadcasting than he pretended, certainly more than many senior executives. He had the quality of loyalty to his staff. He also had a gallant old Austin 12, 1930 or thereabouts, which he drove with great zest, his feet firmly planted on all three pedals simultaneously. He was generous in giving lifts, but a substantial proportion of the space was usually occupied with garden produce or tools or turves, and many an elegantly-dressed secretary arrived with him in the morning a little pale, after a journey in the close company of a bag of evil-smelling fertilizer. In the evening he was liable to stop his car in the middle of the traffic chaos of Mutley Plain, press a ten shilling note into your hand, and ask you to slip out and buy a paper. Squealing brakes, furious drivers, irritated newsboys, alarmed pedestrians, but somehow you got the paper, and Stafford drove on, unmoved, glancing at it from time to time. He had, incidentally, once opened an innings with W. G. Grace, when Grace was old and Stafford was young. The only remark Grace addressed to him was, 'I call everything.'

Characters: Federico de La Iglesia, Victor Stephens, Joan Rendell, R. S. Stafford. I have already mentioned Keith Hamilton Price, who was living at Thurlestone in those years, in a cottage by the sea, with his wife Brenda (Hamilton). Keith is a man who has never ceased to astonish me. He has had at least five careers, all successful. Before the war he was a stage actor, and had reached a West End lead when the theatres closed in 1939. Pictures of him in those days show a svelte matinée idol, some way removed from the vast, genial bulk of today. During the war he became a producer, held high office in ENSA, worked with Basil Dean on a royal command performance, and suffered a breakdown in his health which made it necessary for him to have a quieter life and country air. So he and Brenda went to Thurlestone, and he earned a living as a University extension lecturer in drama, and as a radio actor. Later he became a radio news reporter, and finally moved to Bristol and took up a post in the administration of News and Talks. Although considerably past the normal age of recruitment he became a member of 'established staff', the BBC's accolade. It is an invigorating experience to catch Keith in full conversational flow, behind a pint (well, it used to be pints), his eyes seamed with the wrinkles of a man who laughs a lot, his little-boy grin when he is being mischievous, his tummy quivering with mirth as he approaches the point of a story. He would have been, I believe, a tremendous stage actor if his health had not let him down. He was a good enough radio actor, but could not gain the full effect of his majestic presence in sound alone. At the time he was an announcer (yet another career) he conquered his early difficulties by the simple device of *acting the part* of an announcer; just as he had become an admirable lecturer to adult classes by acting the part of a lecturer, and just as more recently he made the administration work by acting the part of an administrator. If you were to put Keith in an open boat in the middle of the Pacific, he would reach safety simply by acting the part of Captain Bligh.

Frank Gillard is a remarkable man. No doubt he is a man of contradictions. He was then utterly dedicated to West Region, and many years later he was accused of being its destroyer. I expect he always thought he was acting in the best interests of all concerned, and my own experience of working for him was singularly happy. He made us proud of the Region, he made us feel he was proud of us, and we were certainly proud of him. Yet he was a withdrawn man, and his bright blue eyes could be cold. I sometimes thought he was a Venusian – there was a science-fiction story about the Venusians taking over Earth, gradually occupying the key positions in preparation, and it was only their eyes that could give them away. These were passing thoughts, to be brushed away with a laugh. Nobody foresaw what was to come, not even Frank, though even then he would sometimes talk of developments in local radio in America. *But I do nothing upon myself, and yet I am mine own Executioner.*

Employees of the BBC used then to speak of the 'Corporation', or the 'Corp'. Even the abbreviation had a dignified ring. Now it is the 'Beeb', and the verbal change tells you much. The BBC used to claim, or at any rate used to like it said, that it was the best employer in the world, and in many respects it probably was. As I have reason to know, it could be loyal and forbearing to wayward employees (but talent does often take the by-roads). It was commonly said that the only way to get the sack was to seduce the Controller's wife or urinate on the steps (one of these feats I achieved). Yet the BBC could be stubborn and unreasonable, and there were those who, failing to get the sack, resigned in despair. Robert

Waller was one. His novel, *Shadow of Authority*,[1] shows the stuffier side of the BBC in that period. Maurice Gorham wrote, 'The BBC may be a Good Thing or a Bad Thing for the British people, but it is well worth working there if you don't expect security, don't take your work too seriously, don't rise too high, and don't stay too long.'[2] He wrote that in 1948, in what the old hands still look back to as the BBC's golden evening.

What did tend to happen in that post-Reithian era was that the duller, less original men, who were never in trouble because they made no mistakes; who made no mistakes because they never, if they could help it, took a decision; who sat tight and allowed the tides of opinion to wash around their feet – that these were the men (few women then) who ultimately rose to the high positions in the Corporation. Ask no questions, as one of my less respectable aunts used to say, and you'll never get your arse tanned. Too much ability did finish in the rough, while a good deal of mediocrity plodded straight up the fairway. This was the fault of the old-style BBC. Whether it was better than the modern system, with all those whizz kids – chests that would surely ring like gongs, smiles all teeth, computerized brains – it is hard to say. Both systems have had their advantages.

Broadcasting still continues from Bristol and Plymouth, and although autonomy has gone and a regional producer cannot originate a programme without London authority, the hallmark of the west still, I like to think, means something. How long this can last, with regional radio producers increasingly reduced to office-boys for London, is another matter. (The Natural History unit, still based at Bristol, is a fortunate

1. Jonathan Cape, 1956.

2. *Sound and Fury: Twenty-One Years in the BBC.* Percival Marshall, 1948, p. 246.

exception.) To echo Maurice Gorham in at least one respect, it has been well worth working there. In Plymouth, we used to pride ourselves that we were a radio station before Bristol (the old BBC premises in Plymouth were in Athenaeum Street, above a brothel, and there was supposed to have been a Terrible Incident when Lady Astor once opened the wrong door). In fact, the oldest BBC station in the south and west was at neither. Under the 1922 agreement between the British Broadcasting Company (which represented the principal manufacturers of wireless apparatus) and the Postmaster-General, eight broadcasting stations were to be set up: London, Manchester, Birmingham, Glasgow, Aberdeen, Cardiff, Newcastle – and Bournemouth. Nowadays there is no station at Bournemouth, and though there is a studio nearby there is a firm reminder on the table: 'Please remember to refer to this as the *Poole* studio.'

But Bournemouth was first in the field. Its first director was Bertram Fryer, who came from the theatre. He had been director at Newcastle before going to Bournemouth, and he was so popular in the north that when he moved the sale of valve sets in county Durham soared – his admirers adding extra valves in order to pick him up all the way from the south coast. Those were the days when everyone in broadcasting was a man-of-all-work, administrator, producer, broadcaster, and preferably engineer all in one: very like a local radio station today.

Here is the organizer of programmes in that first year, C. A. Lewis, describing the complicated procedure by which the various stations made their separate contributions, and what we would now call their networked contributions, to the general pattern: it is 'a sort of glorified "happy families", where everyone is asking everyone else what they have got or what they want. "Have you Mr Bones, the butcher?" "No, but can you give me the Savoy Orpheans at nine-forty-five?" ' He refers to the labours of Mr Rice, secretary to the company. 'I believe the number of cheques sent off every week from the secretary's department borders on four hundred, but the strain . . . leaves Mr Rice quite untroubled.' When the BBC had been going for a year there was a birthday party. This was notable for a stirring performance by P. P. Eckersley, the chief engineer. To show that he was a man of parts, he 'elected to conduct the orchestra. He did so, breaking two batons, two chairs, the conductor's dais, upsetting all the music on to the floor, and finishing up with the stub end of the baton behind his ear!' 'It was,' Lewis adds to make the point clear, 'excruciatingly funny.'[1] Even the managing director was 'helpless with uncontrolled laughter'.

The managing director was J. C. W. Reith, JOHANNES REITH who confronts us every time we enter Broadcasting House. I do not expect that in later years he was often helpless with uncontrolled laughter. All the glory was still to come, and as the glory came the fun was bound to depart. Perhaps it was a primitive sort of fun. But I have often thought how I would like to see, in modern times, the Engineer-in-Chief conducting the orchestra *à la* Eckersley, and the Director-General holding his sides, as he dodged the flying batons.

1. *Broadcasting From Within.* Newnes, 1924.

9 Babel

In 1953 I decided to try my luck as a freelance. I was far from discontented with my job, but I was, as always, hard up; and at that time any promotion within the BBC would have meant promotion away from the microphone. I was only a little better than an average producer, and had no conceivable talent as an administrator; but I had discovered I could broadcast a bit, and it seemed sensible to concentrate on the thing I could do best. (Nowadays the BBC offers contracts, and even staff posts, to broadcasters; but at that time it was understood that, apart from a few special categories, notably announcers, members of staff did not broadcast themselves – a rule with a lot to be said for it.)

So I chanced my luck and have never really regretted it. As my exuberance and energy diminish I sometimes think wistfully of the security of a quiet, pensionable job; but I have had some much more interesting times than I could have expected had I stayed on the staff; a better run for my money, and better money for my run.

I have broadcast in such an assortment of programmes between 1953 and the present time that I find it difficult to assess them. But there are three aspects on which I shall dwell a little: record programmes, sports programmes and religious programmes. I deal with religious programmes first, because they were the most important to me (or so I would say to myself, and the BBC fortified the pretence by paying for them very badly, thus stimulating a sense of vocation).

The programme I valued most, and which I usually did best, was 'Sunday Half Hour'. I quite enjoyed 'Songs of Praise', the television version; but of all human activities hymn-singing is that best heard and not seen (especially when the singers know they are observed). We have televised news, even though its presentation is dictated by whatever bits of film happen to have come in, because otherwise a large section of the population will never hear any news. We have televised symphonies, or nobody will know about symphonies. So runs the argument. So must we have televised hymns, or people will never know, poor things, that hymns exist. If hymns are dull, then we must pep them up, or pop them up. This is not an approach likely to get the best out of hymns, an art form which can be both delicate and searching; a religious form of antiquity and grace.

'Sunday Half Hour', suffering no visual demands, contrived to keep its integrity as well as its popularity. Indeed, when the planners switched it from 8.30 on a Sunday evening to 10 there was so spontaneous an outcry that they had to change it back. I first introduced the programme in 1949. I did so then, only because my father had died a few weeks earlier. He was due to broadcast a service from the Totnes United Free Church, a prospect which was an excitement and delight to him, but he died a few weeks too soon. So the service was cancelled, and a 'Sunday Half Hour' broadcast instead, a little later. It was therefore by chance that I was connected with the programme in the first place, but one thing led to another, and since then I have introduced it perhaps a hundred times, in a variety of places for a variety of producers.

At that time 'Sunday Half Hour' was usually a jolly sing-song and not much more. The congregation would file in a short while beforehand, belt out their eight favourites, and trot happily away. The comments between the hymns were confined to a quick word or two about the author or composer, a reading of the first line, or verse, and an announcement of the numbers in an assortment of books, which was expected to include *Ancient and Modern*. It was Martin Willson, the Religious Broadcasting Organizer for the West Region who was chiefly responsible for changing this haphazard state of affairs. His early death was a grievous loss to religious broadcasting. He was a pioneer of many ideas which now seem commonplace, but then broke new ground. He felt that 'Sunday Half Hour', with its advantageous placing in the schedules, offered an opportunity for the Christian message which was not being fully used. Because of the appeal which hymn-singing still has for all sorts of people, and because the programme was broadcast on the Light – which was then the programme left on in pubs and motor cars, as well as homes, often irrespective of content – here, thought Martin, was a chink through which a glimpse of the faith might be brought to the many listeners who would scarcely bother, normally, to give it a thought.

It followed that the words of the hymns must be as distinguishable as possible. This required that the singing should be led by a carefully rehearsed choir, or group of choirs, and not just left to an amorphous congregation. It also followed that the introductions to the hymns must mean something: words and music had to be linked together in a common theme, so that the whole programme carried a coherent, if simple message. It did not mean that the spoken links would necessarily be longer, but they would have to be written with care. Since not all preachers are good broadcasters (rather the opposite, because the techniques are so different) this might often mean using professional broadcasters to introduce the programme. Yet broadcasting skill was not enough in itself – an impersonal announcer would not do: the introducer must be able to write his own script.

Martin went to great lengths to try to ensure that all those taking part in the enterprise were conscious of sharing in an act of Christian witness. This may sound obvious, but it is not an easy thing to do in a broadcast, especially in those days when any broadcast, even on sound radio, was regarded as a great event, and when technical equipment was more obtrusive and cumbrous than it is now.

This new approach was not at first very popular with either the BBC or the churches. For one thing, it meant more work by everyone concerned. Then clearly we had to *begin* with the choice of a theme, and this restricted the choice of hymns, and probably cut out some local favourites. It was also upsetting for some churches that a beloved minister might be, as it seemed, excluded from his own pulpit, and a 'man from the BBC' intruded. But tact and usage gradually eased such problems.

It was interesting to see the public response to the new kind of 'Sunday Half Hour' which Martin (and soon several others) produced. The number of letters received was much the same – the programme has always had a large mail. Their content, however, changed. Instead of people writing 'Thank you for some lovely singing', they might say 'Your programme helped me at a difficult time', or 'I've never really thought about the meaning of that hymn before'. These were the letters that pleased Martin, and made him feel that the job was being done.

I have written about Martin Willson's activities in this particular programme because it was one of those in which I was concerned myself. I could give other examples of his fresh and courageous thought. Much of what then was new is today commonplace. There was even a series called 'Eight Five Spiritual', an early experiment in religious pop (the big pop music programme of the time was called 'Six Five Special'). It differed from modern programmes of this kind because, although it used pop music and pop singers, the religious content was much more explicit.

It is doubtful, of course, whether there ought to be such a thing as 'religious broadcasting', with special departments to run it. The term has in practice largely meant 'Christian broadcasting'. One result has been that people working in the religious department sometimes have an uneasy feeling that their position is unjustified, and try to ease their consciences by offering undogmatic programmes, emphasizing the entertainment aspects, with an eye to the ratings, and providing a vague mystical or social content. Attractive, well-made programmes some of them have been, but it is not really the function of religious broadcasting to give people cosy feelings, though there is nothing wrong with cosy feelings. It is not its function to make converts, though it is all to the good if it does; its true function is to explain what Christianity is about (and other religions too, where there is a need). I am coming increasingly to think that religious bodies should be treated much as political parties: given a share of the air and left to get on with it. You know where you are, for instance, with 'Hour of Revival' and Eric Hutchings. I shared in a 'Sunday Half Hour' once with Eric Hutchings, and I remember an admirer calling him, a touch extravagantly, 'England's answer to Billy Graham'. My religious views are some way removed from his, but in his radio programme he buys his time and says what he wants to, and at least the message is clear and the broadcast vigorous. Or take the Daily Service at 10.15 in the mornings, latterly changed to 10.30: an improbable hour for matutinal devotions, but in the days before the war broadcasting on the BBC began at 10.15 in the morning, and it was considered proper, as in any well-run public school, to begin the day with chapel. So the Daily Service has stayed, fossilized among later strata of rock. Yet this too is more than a curious survival: it sets out to do a simple job, and does it.

I have many happy memories of programmes shared with Martin Willson, and his colleague Kenneth Savidge – who extended Martin's ideas into television – and his successor Colin James, now the Holy Father of the Concrete Jungle, the Bishop of Basingstoke. Colin James, when I first knew him, was an earnest, fastidious, compassionate, pink young parson, who liked liturgy and tradition. He copped it properly the night we did 'Sunday Half Hour' with Eric Hutchings in the Colston Hall, Bristol. This vast hall was full, and the singing had been splendidly led by the London Crusader Choir. After I had announced the last hymn I slipped quietly away, knowing what was to come, and went round to the local for a pint, where Colin had optimistically promised to join me. My part was done, and once the hymn was over Eric Hutchings would pronounce the benediction. This he did. Out went the red light. Colin James was prepared to say the few words of thanks customary for a producer on such occasions. Before he could do so, Eric Hutchings, not the man to let an audience of that size get away in a hurry, asked 'our brother James' to lead them in prayer. Our brother James, whose experience of extempore prayer before a couple of thousand experts was perhaps limited, did his stuff, but could hardly proceed directly from 'Amen' to 'And now may I thank you all very much . . .' Hutchings was in the saddle again, launched into a full, powerful, 45-minuter, in the best deutero-Graham style. Colin, paler than usual, arrived just as the landlord was calling 'Time', but I had his pint ready for him, and he drank it as well as I have ever seen any bishop drink a pint. 'Interesting experience,' he said. Like many episcopal remarks, the words would bear a weight of commentary.

There was a trying 'Sunday Half Hour' from Martock, in Somerset. It ought to have been all right. We had had a successful rehearsal in the afternoon: choir tuneful, congregation lusty. All went well in the evening until we came to the third hymn, one of Isaac Watts's best –

The heavens declare thy glory, Lord,
In every star thy wisdom shines

– to be sung to *Winchester New*, a noble tune. I announced the hymn. The organist turned over two pages in his script, something that might happen to anybody, and struck up the equally noble tune *St Magnus*, which we were due to sing later. It is the almost universally used tune to 'The head that once was crowned with thorns'. Away went choir and congregation with a will: but they struck a snag at the end of the second line –

The heavens declare thy glory, Lord,
In every star thy whizz

was how it went. The organist had not realized his mistake, and plunged on. I ran across to him, but he had the swell pedal down and the diapasons out, and I could not make myself understood. Some of the congregation decided to sing *The head that once*, some of them tried to switch to the correct tune, but most of them valiantly went through all five verses of a long metre hymn to a common metre tune. If you have not heard this happen, you can scarcely imagine the effect. Two hymns later, of course, there was *The head that once* looming up again. While Kenneth Savidge, who had rushed into the church from the outside broadcast point, conferred eagerly – I think that would be the word – with the organist, I carried on with the introduction to the next hymn. It was decided that we should leave out *The head that once* and if need be underrun. But it was now my turn to lose my head. In a kind of fascinated palsy, I heard myself announcing the hymn as originally scheduled. The organist, determined not to be caught napping twice, immediately struck up with *St Magnus*. I have never felt quite the same since about either of those hymns.

Perhaps there is one more thing that I may fairly say about my experience of 'R. B. department', even though it has changed so much and can hardly have long to go. Their methods of staffing have often been bad. To be a good producer, whether in sound radio or television, requires some technical ability, a readiness to learn, and about five years. Producers who think they have learnt it in less are – probably – being carried by their programme assistants. The idea that a parish priest can go into the BBC for a few years, and then return to a parish ('his real work', as I once heard Bishop Cockin describe it) has been, and still is, responsible for many feeble broadcasts. It must be recognized that a man may have a call to Christian broadcasting, as he may have a call to the mission field, or monasticism, or whatever: and that if the Holy Spirit testifies to the truth of his calling (the old Dissenting phrase again) he must make it his life's work (or a good part of his life's work: I do not deny the values of variation from time to time). It ought not to happen that a producer returns to parish work, possibly under ecclesiastical pressure, just when he has learnt to begin to make a real contribution to the medium. The average producer is paid much more than the average parson, and no doubt this influences both those who have the jobs and those who have not. 'Well, thank you very much, a very valuable few years' work, but isn't it about time you were thinking of moving on?' Buggins's turn. Martin Willson suffered some obloquy and distress, because he did not return to a parish when some fellow-churchmen thought he had had a good bite at the plum. Indeed return he would have done, had not Frank Gillard shown a proper irritation at the prospect of losing a producer who was just beginning to realize his potential.

Kenneth Savidge, as a layman, faced different problems. As a young man he was convinced that he had a call to some kind of religious work, but doubted if it was to the direct ministry. He tried several different jobs, not very happily or successfully, and in the end took a junior post as an Assistant Studio Manager in the BBC. This brought him to Plymouth, where he soon became more to me than a genial companion. A series of chances led to his becoming Martin Willson's assistant: his vocation had found him after all. We thought this was a considerable achievement by the Holy Spirit. However, Kenneth could not succeed to Martin's position when Martin died because he was a layman. We had a very good successor to Martin in Colin James, but Kenneth's career became diversified and a little thwarted, and ultimately his job disappeared with the West Region. He was appointed successively to posts in Libya and Pakistan, helping to get the television services of those countries going. In each case he arrived in nice time for a revolution, and during the war in Bangladesh fell seriously ill and was lucky to survive. He is now working in an administrative post for the overseas services in London, which cannot inspire him much; but I dare say the Holy Spirit has not done with him yet. He has had a spell as 'Acting' Religious Broadcasting Organizer in Belfast, drawn to the sound of gunfire again. All the same, it seems a ridiculous waste that such a man is not fully employed in religious broadcasting, when you think of some of those who are.

10 Tin Pan Alley

In 1951, I received a letter from Frank Gillard which began, 'I have a proposition which will certainly surprise you.'

He suggested that I should take over as compere, or disc jockey as it was soon to be called, of a West Regional programme called 'What's Your Fancy?' (how the name dates it!) in which listeners' record requests were played. The general musical range was lowbrow to middlebrow. I thought it might be fun, but did not wish to be distracted from what I considered more important matters. I accepted rather pompously, with the proviso that I could give it up in six months if I wished. I was to be a disc jockey, with a few brief interruptions, for the next fifteen years, with never less than one programme a week, and sometimes two.

In 1955, when 'What's Your Fancy?' had been going – so far as I was concerned – for four years, I felt that I had had enough. I was by this time a freelance, but the West Region always looked upon their regular freelances as members of the family, so I had a chat with Bill Coysh, the Assistant Head of Regional Programmes. Bill is a man who ought to appear in my tale more often, for perhaps more than anyone he was the man who kept West Region ticking cheerfully over for half a generation, but he is an unobtrusive man, who did good by stealth. He was the best kind of BBC administrator in the old style: far from a whizz kid. He would not be attracted to the work today.

Bill agreed that someone else should take over the programme. Nor was there any difficulty in finding a successor, for Derek Jones had recently settled in the west. He had had wide experience of broadcasting overseas, and possessed a natural ease at the microphone which I have never known surpassed. He had put a severe illness behind him, and was intent on making a new career. This was obviously a good opportunity to make use of him.

Frank Gillard had now been succeeded as Head of Regional Programmes by Desmond Hawkins, and it was Desmond who amiably threw a spanner. He decided that 'What's Your Fancy?' should come to an end. But the region still needed a record request programme, and this need was to be met by a programme to be broadcast, live, at 8.15 in the morning of every Friday. (It began on Fridays. It moved to other days and became finally established on Saturdays, but it was always a weekly programme.) There were to be two comperes, Derek and I, and the programme was to be unscripted: no formal introductions between the records, just happy chat.

Neither of us was very pleased. Derek was deprived of the programme of his own to which he had justifiably looked forward, and I was deprived of my manumission from records. A trial run on a closed circuit confirmed our forebodings. But we went on the air on Friday, 2 December 1955; and the programme continued almost without interruption until the autumn of 1966, when it drew to a cheerful, champagned close with our own agreement. In its latter years the *Western Daily Press* called it 'one of the great institutions of the West Country'.

It was an unexpected development in my life. But since it was through this programme that I acquired most of whatever reputation as a broadcasting 'personality' I have ever possessed; and since it was so large a part of my life for so long; and since, to be honest, I think it was a pretty good programme of its kind, I would like to consider it for a while.

I had had some differences of opinion with Frank Gillard

about 'What's Your Fancy?' I experimented without a script, equipped only with the request cards, letting the moment provide the exact words. He did not much like this. It is hard to recall how, even as late as the mid-fifties, there was this suspicion of unscripted live broadcasting (no doubt we have now gone too far the other way). Although it was recognized that some programmes – 'Any Questions?', the Brains Trust, any running commentary – had to be unscripted by their nature, the general view was that to broadcast without a script when it was possible to have written one was a needless risk, and probably a sign of idleness as well. It is of course the price that has to be paid for a spontaneous programme that things are sometimes said which would have been better left unsaid, and there were times when this happened to Derek and me. However, Desmond Hawkins took the responsibility of launching us, scriptless, on the early morning air, and it was a responsibility he never shirked, though sometimes he looked as if it was making him wilt a bit. But after a few months he had the public on his side.

What were we to call the programme? We laboured long in vain. Our first producer was Roy Richard Arthur Bernard Hayward, who for some inscrutable reason has always been known in the BBC, which he has served in many capacities, as 'Willum'. After one more fruitless conference, as we were breaking up (it was closing-time, no doubt), Willum said despairingly, 'Oh, why don't we call it some obvious and stupid name, like 'Good Morning'?' So 'Good Morning' it was. And we found a recording of the tune by the London Dance Studio Orchestra, which was used as a signature, and which stood the strain of the years as anything more slick or sophisticated would not have done.

In the early months it was considered essential that we should work from different studios, Derek in Bristol and I in

Plymouth. Difficulties soon arose, since we both had other commitments which often required us to be away from base on Saturdays. It was felt that in these circumstances one or the other of us (but not both) should be replaced for that particular programme. Bernard Fishwick was our first stand-in, and in my view remained the best, though over the years for one reason and another many tried their hands. It was soon realized that it did not much matter where we were, so long as there was a microphone within reach. When I moved to Bristol we were more often than not in the same studio. At one time and another we broadcast from more than twenty different studio centres, as well as such places as the station platform at Blandford Forum, H.M.S. *Eagle*, cricket grounds, show grounds, anywhere convenient; from Paris, Dublin, Edinburgh, the Channel Islands. One summer when I was in Moscow it was intended I should make my contribution from there, but the Russians could hardly have been expected to accept an unscripted programme, let alone this one. They would have argued that the jokes were so feeble they *must* be in code. We broadcast from hospitals and holiday camps and radio exhibitions. Once, when it was all the fashion to set up unusual walking records, I spent the forty-five minutes walking from Broadcasting House, Plymouth, to the Hoe, carrying a watering-can and a current copy of *Bradshaw*. I still hold the world record for this distance in these conditions. People listening to the programme popped out and brought me cups of tea *en route*.

On that occasion Derek was going to take a parallel walk from Broadcasting House, Bristol, to the Clifton Suspension Bridge, but he was ill, and Bernard Fishwick refused to be tempted from the studio. Illness, holidays, a general election and one or two other stray things did cause some brief interruptions in our partnership, but one or the other of us was always there, and I take leave to say, with respect and thanks to the deputies, that the programme was never quite so good – or so bad, if you could not stand it, and there were some who could not – as when we were together.

Practice helped, but there was more than that. A curious mental correlation grew between Derek and me. It was not strictly telepathic. It was just that we learned how one another's minds worked, so that we began to sense, without thinking about it, when to speak and when to pause; when to try for a gag, as our jargon had it, and when to refrain; when to lead the conversation, and when to follow. Desmond Hawkins once said that, in broadcasting terms, he considered me to be an 'attacker' and Derek a 'counter-puncher'. There is something in this, though the image of conflict it suggests is false. There was no rivalry in the programme. We did not know each other particularly well when it began, and since we lived so far apart often did not see much of each other for long periods, until I moved to Bristol, by which time the programme was in its ninth year.

Partly, though only partly, the partnership flourished because of a shared sense of humour. The humour of 'Good Morning!' was usually feeble, I dare say, and the kind that looks even feebler in print. It was conversational humour, and in the conversational joke everything depends on timing and inflection. Consider Sydney Smith. Those who knew him asserted that he was the greatest wit of his day. Yet to read about him is to be stirred to more than a mild smile only occasionally. Sydney was a well-built man, and when he was leaving Bristol, of which he had been a Canon, he turned at the top of Knowle Hill, cast his eyes over the city, placed his hand on his stomach, bowed, and declared, 'Farewell, Bristol. I go, but I take with me the fat of the land.' It sounded very funny when I gave the line to a good actor in a radio play.

Of course Sydney Smith had the advantage of being known as a comic turn. His audience was prepared for laughing, an advantage which Derek and I gradually acquired. As W. S. Gilbert said, 'An accredited wit has only to say "Pass the mustard" and they roar their ribs out.' We became known as 'those two funny men on Saturday mornings'; or, not always unkindly, 'those two fools on Saturday mornings'. We were not sure whether we liked these descriptions or not – were there not many other more important things for which we felt we should be famous? Yet I remember that some years after the programme had ended, at the Tangyes' in Cornwall, I met Carole Carr. She had been one of the raging beauties of my youth, unutterably yearned-for and distant. She still looked radiant and dashing at Dorminack. We had conversed vaguely for about half an hour, when she suddenly cried out, 'Oh! I know you now. One of those Saturday morning fools!' How I glowed.

We depended greatly, in 'Good Morning!' on the 'in' joke. By this I mean something rather different from the 'company' joke, which in broadcasting terms means a joke aimed at someone or something within the firm, and only fully comprehensible to others within the firm. The BBC used to frown severely on this and we were several times in trouble for it. But if you make a company joke often enough it ceases to be obscure. Your regular listeners become aware of the reference, and rather relish the feeling, however spurious, of being on the inside. It might be conversely supposed that new listeners switch off because they cannot understand what is going on. Sometimes this may happen, but if the programme has any kind of gumption to it I think just as many will listen again, so that they can begin to find out.

The audience for 'Good Morning!' was made up mostly of regulars, who frequently provided their own variations on the staple themes. It was our habit, I cannot really remember why, to address one another in the programme as 'mate'. One week we began,

D.J.: Good morning, mate.
A.G.: Good morning, mate.
D.J.: Lovely morning, mate.
A.G.: It is a lovely morning mate.
D.J.: I say, mate.
A.G.: Yes, mate.
D.J.: I've got a letter here from someone who – well, mate –
A.G.: Go on, mate.
D.J.: She objects to us calling one another mate, mate.
A.G.: Ah, well, it only goes to show – one man's mate is another man's poison.

(Signature tune)

An 'in' joke; and also a pun, which was the second staple of 'Good Morning!'

I am prepared to defend the pun. It has been used by many of the masters. It is arguable that it is the only genuinely original form of humour, since it can arise unpredictably from an unpredictable situation. Take away that situation, and it is dead. It can never have been made before, unless exactly that situation has arisen before, and it can never be made again, unless that situation recurs. When he had captured Scinde, Ellenborough telegraphed the word '*Peccavi*'; and Dalhousie capped it, when he had taken Oude, with '*Vovi*'. In the same way, though other puns must have been made on the words 'mate' and 'poison', the particular one I instance could not have been made without a radio programme in which two men were in the habit of calling one another 'mate', which caused a listener to write saying she disliked the habit. It was not a very funny pun, but it was original.

Compare the pun with the joke. It is often said that there are only three basic jokes. That puts it too strongly, but a great many jokes do rely on a small number of ludicrous situations, and by re-jigging the characters, setting, phraseology, they are made to do service over and over again. Does anyone ever sit down to invent a joke? They arise because of a comic happening which gets retold, elaborated, exaggerated, transmuted into hundreds of forms. Since men and women do not change much – though their artefacts do – the comic happenings tend to be the same, even if the jokes have to be readjusted for each generation. I have heard a story involving a fast bowler told successively of Larwood, Tyson and Trueman, and I dare say it was told of Brett of Hambledon. In the second world war there was a story of a number of Italians who had been captured by the Australians. The seats of their pants were cut out, their behinds painted blue, and they were returned with a request that they be replaced by an equivalent number of Germans. I think it was Robert Graves who recalled that he had heard the same story in the first world war, only then it was the Portuguese who were the victims of the Germans, and the Australians who were required as substitutes. He traced other versions and concluded that the story was probably as old as war itself. When Arthur C. Clarke describes a twenty-first-century journey to Mars, it is with a true instinct that he makes a member of the crew burst into the traditional ballad of the skies, ' 'Twas on the space-ship Venus.'[1]

It is difficult to be original, then, when telling a joke: but the number of puns is limited only by the number of possible

1. *The Sands of Mars*. Arthur C. Clarke. Pan Books, 1964: a capital piece of science-fiction.

combinations of words, beyond counting. A listener once wrote complaining that he had heard one of our jokes before. The producer wrote courteously back, explaining that it was the policy of the programme to avoid using jokes the ancestry of which could not be traced back before 1900. At one time we had a spot in the programme called 'Chestnut Corner', but it did not last long: a forest is not a good place to display a leaf.

The producer became known as 'Sir', a commonplace ploy in programmes now, though I do believe it was original (and certainly unplanned) then. The running jokes in 'Good Morning!' – those spread over weeks or months – were governed by the listeners. So long as it was obvious from the listeners' postcards that a theme continued to amuse them, we kept it going. As soon as they dropped it, so did we – we had to, since they were providing no material. Thus there was a time when elephant jokes were thought funny, and fly jokes were thought funny, and the railway station at Blandford Forum was thought funny, and the town clocks of Camborne and Highbridge were thought funny, and the public relations officer of Weston-super-Mare was thought funny,[1] and a hundred and one other things were thought funny – for a little while. They came and went: but Sir remained. Never did the listeners tire of Sir. The programme might open,

1. The public relations officer of Weston-super-Mare was Ted Turner. He is a Yorkshireman, and made a fine sight when declaiming, in the best of Bruddersford voices, that 't' sun always shines at Weston; never stops; joost that clouds soomtimes get in t' way', and similar unchallengeable statements. He had a marvellous gift for getting Weston into the news. Each summer he organized competitions in Birmingham, with prizes of holidays at Weston-super-Mare. Then one winter he ran a competition in Weston, the first prize a week's holiday in Birmingham. The second prize was two weeks' holiday in Birmingham. This also, of course, is an old joke, and none the worse for it.

A.G.: Why does a chicken cross the road?

D.J.: Because one rode a horse and the other rhododendron!

Announcer (hysterical with enthusiasm): That's right! It's the Sir Show!

(Tumultuous applause, fading into signature tune)

We worked our way through 'Son of Sir' and 'I was Sir's Double'. Mr Acker Bilk, who was often a welcome guest on the programme, launched the great 'Sir Must Go!' campaign. At that time the BBC was inviting all who listened to the programme on very high frequency receivers to mark their cards 'VHF'. We in turn invited listeners to mark their cards 'SMG', with a much higher response. At places where Sir was believed to be on holiday 'Sir Must Go!' appeared on posters in the local pubs. Some zealous supporters even manufactured SMG buttons. But the counter-attack was swift, and before long we had news of societies formed for the Protection of Sir. 'Why are you always so unkind to Sir?' 'I think Sir's *sweet*.' We had endeavoured to project the image of a ruthless martinet, but the public insisted on regarding him as a large, friendly, shaggy dog. This was doubtless due in part to the shaggy nature of his jokes. Any especially bad joke was attributed to Sir, and some of the attributions were true – for instance,

A.G.: What is the difference between Noah's Ark and Joan of Arc?

D.J.: Noah's Ark was made of wood, and Joan of Arc was Maid of Orleans.

There were several Sirs. Brian Patten, Light Entertainments producer in the west, held the post for longer than all the others put together. The gem I have quoted, however, came not from him but a previous Sir, Kenneth Savidge. When

Kenneth left us to go into religious broadcasting we were confident that we had done much to stimulate and develop his faculty for prayer.

But Brian Patten was the Sir to end Sirs, and, putting aside the jokes, it was remarkable that he kept us together so happily for so long. Not that we came to dislike each other, or even dislike the programme. We could be sentimental about it. Occasionally we would end with the Dean Martin/Jerry Lewis record of 'Pardners', and we would join in the last chorus.

> You an' me
> We're gonna be pardners,
> You an' me
> We're gonna be pals

And so we were. But we were also professional broadcasters, and this was a job of work. Often people would say 'What marvellous fun you must have on Saturday mornings!' Sometimes we did. When the programme went smoothly, if the records were better than usual, and the conversation clicked along, then it would be true to say that we enjoyed it. But that did not mean we leapt out of bed on a Saturday with a gay 'Hurrah! Another 'Good Morning!' It was more likely to be a resigned, 'Here we go again.'

The music we played tended to become more popular – indeed 'pop', as the word is now understood – as the years went on, which was inevitable in the great pop boom. But we never became, in choice of records, a Radio One-style programme. It is easier to define the programme's record content by thinking of what we did *not* play. Not the classics. Not the light-classical-old-favourites ('Bless this House', 'Love's old sweet song', the Nuns' chorus from 'Casanova'). Not the wilder ebullitions of pop. This left us with more traditional pop, some jazz and modern folk music (not too way out), 'standards' (Sinatra, Ella Fitzgerald) and comedy. As time went on we came to have as many requests for Flanders and Swann, and Bob Newhart, as any other artists.

Once a lady wrote to us with a request for her daughter, implying that they were both regular listeners. The record requested was 'Land of Hope and Glory'. We felt that a regular listener really ought to know that this was the wrong programme on which to request 'Land of Hope and Glory'. So we mentioned the request, apologized for being unable to play the record specified, but linked it with another, 'the nearest thing we had'. The nearest thing we had was 'I'm a hog for you', by Erkey Grant and the Eerwigs. I am happy to say that the ladies saw the joke.

Once or twice attempts were made to see if the Gibson-Jones partnership would work in other settings. We tried a series called 'Good Night', and another on the Light Programme called 'Ad Lib'. I do not think they were bad, but they never completely succeeded. This, I am sure, was because 'Good Morning!' was essentially a cheerful breakfast-time programme, and also a regional programme. Many people outside the south and west listened (we were picked up regularly by an enthusiast at Cape Parry, two hundred miles inside the Arctic circle) but mostly this was because we gave them a reminder of home. The region was not a very big place in terms of population, and this helped to keep the programme on a neighbourly, intimate basis. It was the little local jokes that were liked. People tuned in, I once heard it said, to find out what their friends were up to.

From time to time 'Good Morning!' created rumpuses, the most famous of which was the episode of the Undone Fly, so serious and alarming at the time, in retrospect more comic than credible. When I think of what has happened to the BBC since then I wonder if I can believe my own recollection, but this is the incident as best I can recall it. It happened in 1960. There was at that time a vogue for stories about flies. Thus:

Two flies are playing football in a saucer. One says to the other, 'Practise hard, now. Next week we'll be in the cup.'

A fly buzzes round and round the top of a sealed jam jar. Second fly says: 'What are you doing that for?' First fly: 'Well, it says here, tear round the dotted line.'

Dozens of these stories were sent in, and after a few weeks they palled. I wound them up, at a listener's suggestion, with a quotation from the book of Job. First fly to second fly: *Woe is me, I am undone*. I did not think this very funny, but it was a phrase to fit the moment, and served its turn. I later received a letter from Noel Calvin (q.v.) saying, 'That particular quotation from the prophet was so familiar in that context that I had almost forgotten it had any other.'

The following Monday I received what seemed to me a very severe letter from a senior BBC official, telling me I had gone 'far beyond the bounds of taste', but specifying no details. Truly, I was baffled. I consulted with Jim Smith, the senior studio manager at Plymouth in those days. If you were in any bother at Plymouth it was always wise to consult Jim. He had worked on 'Good Morning!' for years. What, I asked Jim, had I done? After a little effort, he remembered. I had made a passing reference to Scunthorpe, and Jim, ingenious Jim, worked out an interpretation of it which might have been very improper. So clearly the whole thing was a misunderstanding, and cheerfully I rang up the executive concerned to enquire wherein I had offended. He began by sending his secretary out of the room, while he explained. This I thought to be conclusive evidence that it was indeed Scunthorpe that had caused the trouble. Then he told me it was the joke about the undone fly.

I was very angry, and resigned from the programme, which was a stupid thing to do. After a few weeks we had all cooled a little, and there were *amendes honorables*. I add that the executive concerned and I were soon good friends again, because in fact we were, and are. It was a case of tendencies towards pomposity and explosiveness on both sides.

But I hope he will not mind when I say that I shall always cherish the moment when, bless his austere socks, he sent his secretary out of the room, lest she be defiled by the information he had to impart. Did the poor girl stand by the closed door, agog to catch the feverish whispers of vice? (How was she to know that the wretched phrase would be in the national newspapers next day?) She would have had much better value had she, or anyone else, noticed Jim's interpretation of the Scunthorpe *motif*.

There was a further moral to this, which was afterwards recognized. If you are going to take the risk of letting two people loose on an unscripted broadcast conversation, with instructions to try to be funny, you must be prepared for them to make an occasional misjudgement. If the misjudgements become more than occasional, sack them. Otherwise, back them. Nobody could face a programme of this kind if he had always, so to speak, to be looking over his shoulder.

Sometimes, of course, we would land ourselves in a *double entendre* without realizing it. Then we would catch sight of Sir's horror-stricken face and press on, as straightly as we could manage. Once I introduced a request for someone whose name was Mary Lou. Derek said that in this warm weather the loo was a very pleasant place for Mary to be. Slightly paralysed, I hastened on to the record. It transpired that to Derek, a Somerset man, loo simply meant shade, and he was quite unaware of any secondary meaning.

Jim wore a beard, less common then, and had rebellious

views. Come the revolution, he would have seized an aristocrat and a rope, but postponed further proceedings while they argued over interminable pints in the pub on the corner. He left us to join 'Late Night Line Up', which seemed an appropriate transformation. He was a master at manipulating discs and tapes to produce unusual effects. For instance, Ella Fitzgerald made a record of a song called 'Have you met Sir Jones?' Jim removed all the Sirs so that, throughout, she seemed to be singing 'Have you met Jones?' He then removed all the Joneses so that the song became 'Have you met Sir?' Jim produced a marvellous conflation of the BBC announcement of the impending death of George V, against a delicate background of ragtime, with an audience bursting into roars of jubilation at the further announcement that all BBC programmes were closing down. But that we did not include in the programme.

We often referred to Jim's manual dexterity, and as a result some of the studio managers at the Bristol end, determined not to be left out, produced a diverting series of excerpts from the life of one Señor Manuel Dexterité. This in turn produced a letter from the wife of the headmaster of The King's School, Ottery St Mary (where Coleridge's father had been head). She wrote: 'Thank you for giving us Manuel Dexterité for our next term's entry list. We so far have down Luce Chippings, Bill Stickers, Tom Bowler, and we already possess a Primrose Lane.' In turn (this is a good example of the way in which 'Good Morning'! worked) came a spate of similar names from listeners, which kept us going for weeks. Later, I presented the prizes at the King's School, and was delighted to find, apart from Primrose Lane, a very jolly girl called Rosemary Buck, a briskly efficient one called Linda Bussell, and a Rosemary Gollop who was undoubtedly quite a dish. We were bombarded with information about bakers called Bunn, dentists called Payne, and undertakers called Coffin, and in one case (even more sinister) Coughin. Argue and Phibbs, the famous Sligo solicitors, turned up, with a sheet of their note-paper to prove it. All the names were supposed to be genuine, but we had our doubts about one or two, such as the saloon bar fly, Oliver Seamus Hugh Squire (who later, I was interested to see, appeared in a *New Statesman* competition).

Joke broadcasts on 1 April have been overdone in recent years, but we did once experiment successfully. At the beginning of the programme the announcer explained that we were unable to be in our usual studios since, *as many listeners would already know*, we were flying to the United States, to receive the International Disc Jockey Award from Ed Murrow on a coast-to-coast hook-up. But – went on the announcer – in view of the compliment to the BBC, special arrangements had been made for us to introduce the records from a *Comet* high above the Atlantic. The records themselves, of course, would be played in the studio as usual. Well, the studio managers had worked out a very authentic-sounding background, and we had an enchanting air hostess, Valerie (June Barrie). This might not have been sufficient to fool anyone, but after about ten minutes we had a breakdown – contact with the aeroplane lost, embarrassed announcer desperately filling in in the studio, and then contact happily but erratically restored. This did the trick. A very experienced journalist was on the line to the BBC demanding full details. Frank Gillard, West Regional Controller, rang up slightly crossly to ask why he had not been kept informed. Indeed in the end it became a little awkward, because we had a number of kind, congratulatory letters written to us in all seriousness.

We were sometimes in trouble for advertising, another hazard of the unscripted programme, though even in those days the rigidity of the regulations had been somewhat relaxed. Words like 'Hoover' or 'Perspex' will slip out. Once the programme perpetrated two whacking advertisements in a sentence. The culprit was Mr Acker Bilk, who in the course of an interview mentioned that he still carried some Coates's cider in the back of his Bentley. The Coates publicity man was so pleased that he sent us each a bottle. We wrote back, thanking him, but expressing our pained surprise that no Bentleys had turned up. He replied, 'We are working on getting the Bentley account.'

Sometimes we ventured on a little advertising in reverse. Some heavy hints were broadcast to unsatisfactory hotels. When I moved to Bristol I had much trouble getting my new electric door-bell fixed. People from the Electricity Board kept coming and going, deciding where the bell should go, doing the wiring; the bell itself arrived, but lay on the kitchen table, waiting the arrival of the man who should actually put it in position. After some weeks of these delays I consulted Derek, and on the following Saturday 'Good Morning!' cascaded with bells of every description, and an occasional comment upon the efficiency of the Board. The effect was instantaneous. Within minutes of the end of the programme the men arrived, several of them, to install the bell. Unfortunately they arrived at Derek's house, not mine. As he had gone away for the weekend, they had to climb into the house, and were only thwarted by the absence of any bell to install. Mine languished another fortnight. This story sounds so *ben trovato* that I must assert it is strictly true.

We felt we might have adjusted to commercial radio so long as the sponsors did not mind the practice known as 'ribbing the product'. Here is an authentic example, very much in the Gibson/Jones style. The participants were Gene Autry and Bing Crosby.

'Messieurs, ze duel shall begin, and shall end when you hear "touché".'

'What do you mean, "touché"?'

'I mean to shay that Swift's Premier Ham is the only ham that's brown-sugar cured to give it a fine flavour . . .'

I dare say we could have managed that kind of thing, and would have done if anyone had been prepared to pay us to. We were not high-minded in such matters, nor very well paid for the work (though, to be sure, if you are a freelance there is a lot to be said for a regular cheque, even if it is a small one). But as it was I doubt if 'Good Morning!' ever helped to sell anybody anything, unless some entrepreneur set up as a vendor of cold chip sandwiches, a delicacy for which I was truthlessly said to have a passionate attachment (I once had them served on a silver salver at Weston-super-Mare). 'People do not buy from clowns,' said Claude C. Hopkins, the advertising giant: unless, no doubt, it is clownery they are seeking to purchase. The corollary of this was that the impression steadily grew that Derek and I had *only* clownery to offer. We could not spend the rest of our life being the Saturday morning fools. In my case there was the additional complication of political activities, in which my Saturday morning reputation did me no good at all.

The justification for the programme, apart from the fact that it helped us to earn our living, was that a lot of people liked it; and I cannot think it did much harm. Some listeners had a touching devotion. There were others who could not stand it at any price. 'Good Morning!' always aroused extreme opinions. In a small way, considering how record programmes have developed, we were pioneers, though that is not much to be proud of. We did not join in the vogue for satire, except sometimes to satirize the satirists a bit ('This is not so much a way of life – more a programme'[1]). We did not deliberately sail near the wind. We made no great claims for ourselves. When the programme ended, the compliment that pleased us most was a quotation, offered by a listener, from Kipling: 'mirth that has no bitter springs.'

1. This joke was inevitably used by almost everybody, but we were first, the very morning after its first appearance.

11 Lord's and Twickenham

Sir Home Gordon once declared that his idea of bliss in eternity would be to watch a perpetual series of finely contested cricket matches.[1] At the other extreme was a character called John Clegg of the *Manchester Evening News*, who – Sir Neville Cardus has told us – rejoiced openly when it rained.

> Once I arrived late at Old Trafford, after a journey from Lord's. It was the lunch interval, and the scoreboard announced that Lancashire against Northamptonshire had lost five wickets for fifty on a dull morning threatening bad weather. I met Clegg as soon as I had entered the ground and realized the dismal situation of the Lancashire side. 'Looks very bad,' I said to Clegg; but after an inspection of the clouds above he said, 'Too high, I'm afraid, too high.'[2]

There was a time in my youth, extending even to my twenties, when I would have been inclined to agree with Sir Home Gordon. Probably this condition was extended, and exacerbated, by the relatively cricketless war years. There have been times in recent years, when I have been broadcasting or writing about cricket regularly, when I have glanced at the looming clouds, and my thoughts have turned with Clegg's to the refreshment tent.

Cricket has changed, and I doubt if it has changed for the better, but most of the change has been in me. I noticed this very much in 1968, the season I began to write about the game

1. In the opening paragraph of *Background of Cricket*. Arthur Barker, 1939.
2. *Second Innings*. Collins, 1950, p. 178.

for *The Times* as often as five, six or even seven days a week. For twenty years before that I had been broadcasting commentaries from time to time, with an occasional newspaper report, but I found a world of difference between perhaps a dozen matches a summer, thirty or forty days of cricket, and the daily grind. By the end of that season I realized, what in my youth would have been incomprehensible, that county cricketers have reason to feel stale by the middle of August. Since then we have had the rapid development of one-day matches, which have certainly brought variety to the scene. They have occasionally brought farce as well, especially in the Sunday League, but something drastic had to be done if the game was to continue as a professional entertainment. Two three-day county matches a week, played in the modern style, so often grimly cautious, so supposedly scientific, had ceased to be the way to get the best out of the game. One-day matches were the price cricketers had to pay, if they wanted to be able to continue with their three-day championship, even in a curtailed form; and most of the professionals have recognized this, even if they are not enthusiastic about it. No doubt there will be further experiments yet, and it may be that despite them all the three-day county game cannot last very long. If so, I should be sorry (though I should be very glad to see the five-day test match reduced to three). But cricket, as such, is not in decline. More people are playing it, all over the world, than ever before, and that is the only sane way of judging the health of a game.

The other game I have regularly covered is rugby football. I have never had any difficulty in sustaining interest in that, partly because it rarely involves more than a couple of afternoons a week. I will go to a rugby match for fun. I have even been known to pay at the gate. Rugby is also less affected by the weather. It is astonishing that cricket should have taken root in the English climate. It almost makes me believe that our summers have grown worse over the past few centuries, though people who have studied the evidence say it is not so. The weather has often made me rue a cricket reporter's life, as it might be in a May shower of snow at Derby, or when an autumn easterly at Scarborough almost rips you off your seat.

Yet both games have given me much pleasure, and helped me to earn a living, and I am grateful. If I touch on them only shortly in this book it is because I have written so much about them elsewhere, in the course of my daily work.

I have told how the Leyton ground introduced me to cricket. H. S. Altham and E. W. Swanton, in their *History of Cricket*, called it a 'somewhat grimy yet not wholly unattractive enclosure which had brought all the great cricketers, in their time, to the East Londoner's doorstep.'[1] So it did, and in the early thirties I suppose I saw them all, except Bradman, who did not play when the 1930 Australians were there.

Whenever Yorkshire came I reminded my school friends of my northern origins. There was not much risk of Yorkshire failing to live up to my faith, and there was one unforgettable day in 1932, when Holmes and Sutcliffe opened the Yorkshire innings and put on 555 runs together. That was then the record for any wicket anywhere, and is still the record for the first wicket anywhere, and for any wicket in England. The previous record (Brown and Tunnicliffe's 554, also for Yorkshire, at Chesterfield in 1898) was passed shortly before lunch on the second day, so I was home from school in time to watch it from the balcony.

There was an odd incident at the end of the partnership, of which I have since read several contradictory accounts. When the scoreboard moved to 555 there was much cheering, and Holmes and Sutcliffe strode down the pitch towards one

1. Allen and Unwin, first published 1926.

another and shook hands. Sutcliffe had a carefree swing at the next ball and was bowled. Yorkshire at once declared. Then the two scorers disagreed about the total: there was a no-ball in one book which could not be matched in the other. The scoreboard reversed to 554. Indeed, Holmes and Sutcliffe were photographed under it, at that figure. They had only equalled the record, not broken it.

By this time I was within the ground, nobody bothering in the excitement to keep out the small boys who thronged at the gates. Some of my schoolmates rejoiced evilly at the tragedy. Ultimately the no-ball was demonstrated to sufficiently general satisfaction, and the board went back to 555 for another photograph; but it was a bad moment. My schoolmates and Essex, however, had a notable revenge a few years later, when Essex got Yorkshire out for 31 and 99 and, scoring over 300 themselves, won by an innings. But by then Essex had left Leyton.

Since they returned there for a week or so a season, a few years ago, they have been well supported. It was at Leyton that an old friend of mine, Carter Dodds (inappropriately called 'Dicky' by cricketers, who have a gift for inappropriate nicknames) had a very successful benefit match. He had not insured against bad weather, believing the event to be within the providence of God. A bad spell cleared just in time. He gave all the proceeds to Moral Re-Armament, a movement of which I do not much approve, but one which he has served for many years with the utmost selflessness.

I did not have the chance to watch cricket at Leyton again myself until 1970, and it was then with some emotion that I walked round the ground. At a glance it was much the same except about half the size my imagination recalled. It is less grimy than it was, and the assorted smells – the soap-works at Stratford, the wire-works by the Marshes – no longer float pungently across. The pavilion is the same, at least from the outside (I had never been inside before), a very decent piece of cricketing architecture. There used to be some big three-stepped rough stone seating for the general public, solid as the rock of Gibraltar and trying to tender behinds. That too had gone, and it must have been a formidable job to shift it.

There is now a handsome new sports centre on the Leyton ground. When Essex left, the ground passed to the Metropolitan Police, and I was particularly cross about having to watch fat policemen run where O'Connor had batted and Farnes bowled. Now it is owned by the borough of Waltham Forest, and in constant use for a variety of sports by many young people. One must be thankful that this patch of green in east London has still survived, and still has the character more of a field than a stadium. But as a consequence the outfield, once renowned for its richness and regularity, is bumpy and bare in places, though the square itself still usually plays well.

Near the Leyton ground there had been a bat-maker's shop, *W. J. Breeden*, which supplied many of the Essex cricketers with bats. Mr Breeden's nephew Bobby lived with him, much of an age with me. I cherished his friendship because he was my nearest contact with the mighty. One day Bobby and I, with some others, had been to Wanstead Flats for a picnic, and on the way back Bobby, throwing my bat in the air, failed to catch it as it fell, and it dropped on the asphalt road. It broke in two, right across the middle. It was nearly new, a Marks & Spencer three-spring driver, 4*s* 11*d* ('Nothing Over 5/–' was their slogan), so the calamity was dreadful. The only hope was that Bobby's uncle would be able to mend it. We hurried to the shop, but uncle shook his head sadly and said, 'Sorry, it can't be done.'

In 1970 I saw the little shop again, unchanged, even to the

picture of the Australian eleven of 1888. I went in, and there, bless me, was Bobby Breeden himself. After a variety of jobs and much travel he had come back to run the family business – 'I had to do it,' he said, 'I was the only Breeden left.' But before that he had said, as soon as I had introduced myself, 'Why, I remember you – I broke your bat!' It seems an inappropriate story to tell of a bat-maker. But beautiful bats are still made in the little shop, and it was moving to find it still there, and still in the family, under the shadow of the big railway arches of Leyton Midland station; only a few yards from what was once one of the most famous cricket grounds in the world.

It was a grief to me that I could not play games better. I was just about good enough to enjoy them, and at school and college acquired by assiduity a fair number of colours, but it became clear quite soon that I was never destined for more than average competence. It is a handicap, in reporting a game, not to have played it at a first-class level; but not an insuperable handicap, as many distinguished names witness. It is certainly desirable, and in nearly every case necessary, to have played the game you are reporting at *some* level, regularly and enthusiastically. But, given that requirement, the same considerations apply to making a sports journalist or broadcaster as to making any other kind of journalist or broadcaster.

From my first experience of cricket commentary at Taunton in 1948 I progressed to covering matches in the western counties, perhaps half a dozen, then a dozen times a season. After about five years I was considered good enough to be invited by other regions sometimes, but it was fourteen years before I was awarded a test match. I suppose I have done more commentaries at Taunton than anywhere, which is no doubt why it is my favourite ground. It is not particularly beautiful, if only because of the huge hoardings put up to stop spectators in the road watching for nothing. But it is comfortable, friendly, compact without being poky. Often in recent years there has been talk that Somerset would leave it, and certainly support has been rather better at Bath. I should be sad if the day came. I should be sad no longer to watch cricket against the background of the Quantocks, of Cothelstone with its quiff of trees. There are not so many county grounds which remind you that cricket was a countryside game. All the same, I had an alarming experience on that first occasion. The commentary box at Taunton in those days was a precarious affair, which looked as though the first puff of a south-westerly would blow it over. To reach it you had to climb a ladder out of the ground, over a wall into the churchyard, and then climb another ladder to the roof of the stand. Keith Miller, when he went in, threatened to knock the whole lot of us down with one blow, and came within a couple of yards of doing it. So my career as a cricket commentator might have been ended before it began: but it would have been a noble ending, I would have thought at the time. To be knocked off the air and into the churchyard by Miller!

Broadcasting and journalism need different talents, just as television commentary and what we now call radio commentary require different talents. Very few people have been good at all three: start counting after you have said John Arlott, E. W. Swanton, and Peter West. Too much radio is done by good journalists – I am thinking less of running commentaries than the short eye-witness accounts. Radio should be conversational, not a newspaper piece read aloud. Equally, too much journalism is done by good broadcasters. Years of gabbling away at two hundred words to the minute spoil an English style. I have been a broadcaster first and a journalist second, and my prose tends to be vague and prolix, rather than precise and economical. (The sentence illustrates the point –

it is the commentator's perpetual temptation to throw in another word, for it keeps you going for another half-second.)

Occasionally I have broadcast about other sports, unconvincingly. Once – it was an emergency, and I was helping out – I broadcast commentary upon an F.A. Cup tie, between Swansea Town and Peterborough United, at Swansea. It was the first soccer match I had seen for at least ten years, and at the end of it I found I had to interview Tommy Docherty, who was there on behalf of Chelsea, who were to play the winners. (The match was a mid-week replay.) 'And what do you think,' I asked him in the usual idiotic way, 'will happen when Peterborough meet Chelsea?' 'There will be a first half and a second half, and eleven men on each side.' 'Oh, splendid,' I said, enthusiastically, not appreciating the nature of the reply until it was too late.

The principal problem of cricket commentary, I have found, is to provide an adequate supply of background information which is both interesting and relevant. If you are fortunate enough to have a scorer, such as Arthur Wrigley or Bill Frindall, in the box, that is an enormous help; but statistics, even if appropriate, are not in themselves enough. There are often long periods in cricket when not very much is happening. Suppose a fast bowler spends five or six minutes bowling to a batsman who is determined to attempt no stroke, and all the balls go down the off side and are taken by the wicket-keeper. It is the ability to keep the commentary going, without obvious padding, without making the listener feel bored, that is needed – it is perhaps this more than any other quality which distinguishes Arlott above all the rest of us. Television commentators do not have this particular problem: a picture of the fast bowler retreating thirty yards, and silence, is sufficient explanation of the situation.

With rugby football, on the other hand, the difficulty in

radio is not to elaborate, but to keep up the pace. When play is fast and open, which happens much more often now than it used to, as a result of the changes in the laws – then the problem is simply getting out the words swiftly and accurately enough to tell people what is going on, without lagging behind the play.

Probably the most important ability in television commentary – some purists have maintained that it is the only important one – is to identify the players. This is not so in radio, and not just because 'the listener can't see'. It is more important to keep up with the play, to say in what part of the field the ball is and why, than to pinpoint a particular player. Not long ago I heard an audition by a young man anxious to take up rugby commentary on radio. He had clearly worked hard beforehand at his homework. His identification of players was quick and almost flawless: out tumbled the names in a long list. But no pattern emerged: as often as not we did not know even which half of the field the ball was in.

I do not want to sound unsympathetic to this young man, indeed I sometimes wish I had half his complaint. But his priorities were wrong. I learnt this in the first rugby commentary I ever broadcast, a county match between Gloucestershire and Cornwall at Bristol. Gloucestershire won the ball from a scrummage on their own twenty-five, their stand-off half waiting for the ball and poised to kick for touch. I forgot his name, took my eyes from the play to glance at my programme, fumbled for a second or two. When I looked up, Cornwall had scored. I did not know how or why. I discovered later that the stand-off had made an air shot, and Michael Terry of Cornwall had booted the ball over the line and touched it down. There were no helpful summarizers or 'No. 2s' in those days. I felt, and sounded, a complete fool. Now I should not have forgotten the player's name, but these things do happen, and when they do the rule is to stay with the game. Listeners will forgive you forgetting a name, even if it is a famous name which they and you know perfectly well: but they will not forgive hearing a triumphant roar from the crowd and a commentator who does not tell them what it is about.

Even so, mistaken identifications are a nightmare, and I am not allowed to forget that once I got Colin Cowdrey wrong. Indeed, I had him out before he had come in to bat, and this at the crisis of a Kent-Hampshire match. There were some extenuating circumstances, but I will not rehearse them. The episode is too painful to me.

Then there are odd, and often inexplicable, mix-ups of words. Once, during a cricket match at Taunton, I informed the public that the ball had gone for two interviews. The word I intended to employ was overthrows. I had no interviews on my mind at the time. I was unaware I had said it, and did not even believe I had said it, until the recording was played back. Another time, Robert Hudson at Lord's, when the teams were presented to the Queen, said, 'What a moment this is for the New Zealanders! A moment they will always want to forget . . .' I hope he will not mind my stealing his story, because I was in the commentary box at the time, and diffidently pointed out to him, afterwards, what he had said; and he did not believe it either, until he had listened to the tape. This story has been retold and elaborated, and attributed to various commentators. There is one charming addition, in which the commentator is made to correct himself: 'I beg your pardon, I mean a moment they will never want to remember . . .' But that is apocryphal, and I can vouch for the original.

Spoonerisms can produce horrifying effects. I notice, however, that they rarely recur in the same form. Once they have been committed an automatic warning signal shows itself. I was very relieved, a few years ago, to hear an announcer refer to the Channel Island of Jernsey. I had been dreading it for years, but now there was the sense that the gipsy's curse was expiated. 'Jernsey' is not strictly a spoonerism, but it illustrates the point. For years I have been hopefully listening for the Bules of Kite, Chank Fracksfield and his orchestra, the well-known sculptor Shamuel Seepshanks, the Society for the Reservation of Plural England, and the famous rugby international John Carnal-Crumpeter. Hugh Shirreff recounts with gusto the occasion when he introduced a concert of mad songs and partrigals. There was another West Regional announcer who took us over to the Bath Room Pump.

A spoonerism, a transposition of the initial consonants of two words, takes its name from the Rev. W. A. Spooner, Warden of New College, Oxford. He died at the age of eighty-six in 1930, and in my Oxford days there were many who remembered and relished him. It is true that he once announced in chapel the hymn, 'Kinquering congs their titles take.' I am less sure of the story that he became engaged to be married when intending to ask a lady if she would make tea, and she did not need asking twice. No doubt they spent the honeymoon in Jersey.

It has been said that the best commentators make the worst mistakes. As a statement that is untrue, and has the ring of someone laughing off incompetence. But a true point labours within the clumsy excuse. The best commentators, in my experience (and obviously I would be lying if I pretended I did not think I was among them) are those who have most trouble in conquering their nerves. It is a good thing to be a little edgy, a little tense – even if you contrive not to show it – before a big occasion. Studio broadcasts I have usually found easier; but a commentary, or any sort of unscripted outside broadcast where you can never tell what will happen next, is always a strain. The tension builds up over the years; sleep is the first thing to go. This is when you begin to drink too much and reach for the barbiturates too often.

Yet with this tension there goes, I have found, immense enjoyment, and, when things go right, immense satisfaction. It is a splendid moment when an invitation arrives for a test match (especially if it is at Lord's) or a rugby international (especially if it is at Twickenham). It was a marvellous experience to broadcast the closing overs of the West Indies test at Lord's in 1963, when, with an over to go, four results were still possible; or to broadcast Devon's win in the county rugby championship in 1957, their first for forty-five years; or the match between Ireland and France at Lansdowne Road in 1969, Ireland's first win over France for ten years; or the University match in the same year, when Oxford, led by Laidlaw, won with thirteen and a half men; or a dozen others, easily recalled. Since my sports reporting has been limited to minority sports I have never had the chance of covering such occasions of world importance as the Olympics; and since sport has never been more than a part of my work I have never been able to go on a winter tour. All the same, when I think of all the fair and happy sporting days when I have actually been paid to be present, I consider myself lucky.

Not that I would wish to become solely a sports reporter. For me, variety is not the spice of life, but the meat.

Also, I am afraid, if I did nothing but report games, I would take them too seriously. Many do. Much scorn has been poured on statements such as 'It doesn't matter who wins, so long as it is a good game.' I have no doubt, however, that that is the right approach. It is natural and harmless, to a point, to let one's emotions become involved in sporting encounters. I suffer a good deal every second Tuesday of December at

Twickenham. But out of all the University matches I may see each side will win about half, and who would seriously have it otherwise? When in 1953 England, at last, won the Ashes at the Oval, an Australian said, with relief, 'Now we can all go back to barracking for Australia.' He used the word 'barracking' simply in the sense of 'cheering on', not in the pejorative sense in which English journalists have sometimes used it.

The solemn, religious approach of Englishmen to cricket – 'DISASTER FOR ENGLAND' on the newsbills, and all the rest of it – is, or ought to be, no more than a kind of ironic joke in which cricketers themselves share. (The trouble with the 'computer test match' in 1972 was simply that joke was pushed too far.) One year, the Lord's test coincided with the Vatican election. Suddenly the two big chimneys on the St John's Wood Road side began to emit huge puffs of smoke. 'Good Lord,' said Brian Johnston, 'they've elected Jim Swanton Pope.' E. W. Swanton takes his cricket seriously, as it is his job to do, and he writes about it with a depth of knowledge and a stern graciousness not surpassed among the cricket writers of his generation. But he knows, and we know he knows, that there are more important things than cricket. One of the best broadcasts I ever heard him make was in the series 'Christian Forum'; and one of the most pungent pieces of his prose I ever have read was a letter to the *Spectator* concerning the immigration question.

I believe (or perhaps all I mean is, I hope) that nearly all the best writers on sport have had interests in other fields, and consequently a sense of proportion. Hazlitt, Darwin, Cardus, Arlott are names which come quickly to mind. In slightly different categories, though still illustrating the point, are Stephen Potter, Robertson-Glasgow, Henry Longhurst. I dare not extend the list, or old friends will justly begin to ask me why they have been left out. It would never occur to any of these men to make a golden calf of sport: but a golden calf it has become, in our society, with thousands of businessmen and television and radio producers, quite apart from the journalists, fighting for their spoonsful of golden calves' foot jelly.

In the brave old days of the *British Weekly*, when under the editorship of Shaun Heron it was the only religious paper a radical could hopefully read, this appeared:

> The sports writers of Britain are a big-headed lot with more than a little of the hysterical about them. They are angry with Lew Hoad because he chose not to tell them what his private plans for his own future were. They were just as hysterical when he got married without telling them. The Biggest Head in Sports Writing, that of Mr ———, of the ———, is quite shocked. It appears that for athletes to be decent people these days they should tell all to the sports writers.
>
> The controllers of 'amateur' tennis are also angry with Mr Hoad – they were also angry when he didn't tell them he was getting married – but he has been good for a lot of people who have no illusions about a game which is pure shamateur and whose rulers rule the players as if they were paying them. Mr Hoad has been a great refreshment for a great many of us. To the arrogant controllers of shamateur tennis and to the egotistical sports writers of Britain he said, 'go jump in the lake and let me mind my own business.' There are few enough people who belong to themselves. When we see them these days we should sing a little song.[1]

It is not one of Shaun Heron's more elegant pieces of prose. It bears the marks of hasty writing, and I do not suppose that

1. *The British Weekly*, 11 July, 1957. I leave the name blank, though it appeared there, because it might prove a conversational diversion guessing who it was.

the Hoad case, whatever it may have been about, was so simple as all that. But I cut out the piece and kept it, as a reminder that sports writers do tend to assume an arrogant priesthood, none the better if they are worshipping heathen gods. Or, in Shaun Heron's livelier metaphor, that the people who actually play the games are within their rights if they tell us to jump in the lake.

For many years I contributed to 'Sport in the West' – latterly known colourlessly as 'Sports Page' – the Saturday evening sports programme from Bristol. In this programme, especially when Anthony Smith was producer, we tried to encourage the natural broadcasters, the natural speakers. Some were journalists and some were not. John Mason was a journalist who rapidly took to the microphone as a friend. I like to think I had something to do with his broadcasting career. Ross Salmon became very good, and so did Gerald Bennett (I am thinking mostly of the rugby reporters). One of many pleasant memories of the programme is that Mollie Gerrard used to broadcast about rugby.

Mollie is the widow of R. A. Gerrard, who played rugby for Taunton School, Bath, Somerset and England. He was in the centre with Peter Cranmer when England beat New Zealand for the first time, in 1936 – and Peter was another admirable broadcasting reporter whom we would use in 'Sport in the West' whenever we could lure him from the midlands, as well as a much under-estimated commentator. When I first went to school at Taunton, there were – so far as we small boys were concerned – three famous Old Tauntonians: M. E. Aubrey, the secretary of the Baptist Union and a Companion of Honour; J. H. Cameron, the West Indian cricketer who had taken 10 wickets for 49 in one innings for the Rest against Lord's Schools; and Gerrard. After the New Zealand match Gerrard was leading Cameron by several lengths, with Dr Aubrey labouring in the rear.

Bob Gerrard was killed in the war, after being decorated on the field at Alamein. I think Mollie's devotion to rugby football is a way of expressing devotion to her husband. Knowing how much he would have done for the game himself had he lived, she has tried to make up the loss as much as she can. In the same way by her work as an architect she has carried on the work of her father. As for the architecture, Bath carries her imprint in a number of places; and it is a particularly testing place to be an architect. She received an award for her rebuilding of the Royal National Hospital for Rheumatic Diseases, which does not sound a very attractive place but was one of the best efforts of John Wood. As for the rugby, her many services to the game, quietly and selflessly done, were crowned in 1971 when she was made President of the Bath club. She has sometimes combined her two interests, building the new stand at Devonport, and rebuilding the old one at Bath. Once she was asked (having lodged a sharp complaint or two) to make a survey of the women's lavatory accommodation at Twickenham. I met her behind the West stand before a big match one afternoon, advancing like an Amazon, waving a broken length of lavatory chain. 'I've got my evidence!' she cried. She is a tall, handsome woman, striking in any company. In the chimney-pot hat era, I was once moved to quote *Alice* to her, and suggest that all persons more than a mile high should leave the court. Outspoken, quite ferocious if she suspects any slur, real or intended, on her beloved husband, she is nevertheless a gentle, gracious person, one of the most loyal of friends. They had only been married eighteen months when her husband went to war. A few hours before he was killed he said to a friend: 'If anything goes wrong, please tell my wife this: if the best man on the side has to leave the field, what you want is a substitute.' But there has been no substitute. I once said to her, foolishly enough, 'You didn't have very long, Mollie, did you?' And she smiled, and said, 'Well, dear, you must remember we didn't waste a minute or regret a minute.' The dead neither give nor are given in marriage, but if personality survives there is something waiting that can only be joyful.

I have more good memories of sports broadcasting from a programme called 'Sporting Fanfare', later changed to 'Sporting Questions'. This ran for some years, first on the West of England Home Service and later on the Light Programme. It was a kind of sporting 'Any Questions?' and as with its mother programme the emphasis was placed on courageous but good-humoured discussion of current problems by articulate men. I was for a while producer of this programme, and for a while chairman. We chose for the teams not, necessarily, the most famous players of games, but the best (I cannot help coming back to the phrase) *conversational* broadcasters. It does sometimes happen, of course, that the best players are also the best broadcasters. Of such was John Kendall-Carpenter, now headmaster of Wellington School, Somerset. He won twenty-three rugby international caps for England, but the number of his caps, or indeed whether he had any at all, was not the decisive reason for inviting him. Denzil Batchelor was often with us. Many years ago Denzil, when secretary to C. B. Fry, was described by James Agate as one of the best talkers he had ever met, and it must have taken a lot to make your mark as a talker when Agate and C. B. Fry were among those present. Often we had John Foot, Peter West (star rising but not then of first magnitude), E. W. Swanton, and J. P. W. Mallalieu. Bill Mallalieu was the best of them all. He had been a rugby blue, but he had not experienced a very fortunate University match. He played at scrum-half, and was twice off-side in lamentable positions,

Cambridge kicking two penalty goals – the margin by which they won. It was this disaster, Jim Swanton would maintain, which turned him away from the paths of grace, so that he joined the Labour party and became the most fanatical supporter of Huddersfield Town. We used to have severe political arguments, Bill and I, but he could always silence me by asking, 'And when are the Liberal party going to put up a candidate for Huddersfield East?' He was the member for Huddersfield East, and at that time the Conservatives gave the Liberals a straight fight in Huddersfield West, provided we did the same for them in East: an arrangement of which a radical could hardly approve, but we were in desperate straits then. I used to threaten to go up to Huddersfield East and stand against Bill myself, and once or twice, at two in the morning, I might even have believed myself.

When I look back on all the broadcasts with which I have been associated, I would choose two moments of the purest joy. One was in an agricultural quiz, with farmers on one side, and representatives of farming industries on the other. One of the latter, who managed a sausage factory, could not get a single answer right. He was a tubby, cheerful Devon character, who did his best to take it all in good part, but his repeated failures were obviously distressing him. It came to the last round. The chairman – McMurtrie – asked him the question, 'What is a heifer?' The manager's round red face split with relief: 'Ah!' he said, 'I think I do know that one, Mr Chairman. A heifer, 'tis a female cow.'

The other, different, was in 'Sporting Questions'. In a programme at Sherborne the team had been asked to suggest some of the outstanding books written on sport. This was what we called a 'preview' question – the team had been given advance notice of it, and the listeners were so informed. There were some types of questions which could be better dealt with in this way, and we always made it clear to listeners when it was done. A number of good suggestions was made: *The Compleat Angler*, *The Clicking of Cuthbert*, de Selincourt's *Cricket Match*, Altham and Swanton's *History of Cricket* were among them. In conclusion, John Foot spoke of Hazlitt as a sports writer – Cavanagh at fives, and the prize fight between Bill Neat and the Gas-man. He read an extract from Hazlitt's account of the battle upon Hungerford Downs, read it in that trenchant Foot voice, and when he had finished the audience (many of them, no doubt, hearing it for the first time) burst into a round of applause which went on so long that we had to cut a good deal of it in the edited version of the recording. This was the passage of Hazlitt which John Foot quoted, when Hickman, the Gas-man, is about to go down:

> I never saw anything more terrific than his aspect just before he fell. All traces of life, of natural expression were gone from him. His face was like a human skull, a death's head, spouting blood . . . He was not like an actual man, but like a preternatural, spectral appearance, or like one of the figures in Dante's *Inferno* . . . Ye who despise the *Fancy*, do something to show as much 'pluck', or as much self-possession . . . before you assume a superiority which you have never given a single proof of, by one action in the whole course of your lives![1]

It was a simple thing, but unforgettable. And it made two points for the tradesmen of sport, whether practitioners or reporters: that sport is not altogether to be despised, and that it has produced much writing which is not to be despised either.

1. 'The Fight', William Hazlitt, first published in the *New Monthly Magazine*, 1821.

12 Cornwall

I have been told, and like to think, that there is Cornish blood in my family, but I am not clear how and whence it came – possibly through miners going north, seeking a more secure living from coal than tin could provide. After all, it used to be said that anywhere in the world, if you found a hole in the ground, you would find a Cornishman at the bottom of it. However that may be, my second wife has an impeccable Cornish ancestry, and now I have a son who can play rugby for the county when he grows up, and a daughter who can criticize him.

I love Cornwall as much as an alien is permitted to do, and especially St Ives. I first was taken on holiday to St Ives in 1934, and go there for holidays still; and there were those years when my home was at Falmouth. Ever since then, through broadcasting, politics, rugby, but most of all through affection, I have had close associations with the county. Some zealots patriotically but mistakenly like to call it the Duchy, but the Duchy of Cornwall is quite a different animal from the county, and includes such diverse bits as Dartmoor Prison and Kennington Oval.

Although I have put most of my sporting thoughts in the previous chapter, I must say something here about Cornish rugby. Nowhere else in England does the passion for the game run so deep. Go into a pub in Redruth or Camborne, and you will hear them talking about 'football': no need for the qualifying 'rugby'.

One of the best moments in sport I remember was in 1967 at the Richmond Athletic Ground, when in the seventh minute of injury time Roger Hosen made a conversion from the touchline, and Cornwall had drawn level with Surrey in the county championship semi-final, after being down 14–3 midway through the second half. Without waiting for the final whistle thousands of Cornishmen raced on to the field, every one of them wearing or flourishing something black and gold, raising a din to wake the Mermaid of Zennor. For hours afterwards the neighbouring streets were like Helston on Furry Day. It was particularly delightful that this should happen at Richmond. 'Can't ever play well at Richmond,' a famous Welsh forward is supposed to have said, 'all that bloody polite clapping.' As the rest of the crowd contemplated the abandoned Celtic fervour their looks could have been described as glazed.

A fortnight later I was on Penzance station the day after Cornwall, unbelievably, had lost the replay at home. All was hushed. Ancient spirits brooded. People went about their tasks reverently, as in the house of the bereaved. 'A grievous day for the county, sir,' said the man selling papers, no trace of humour in him.

I remember, too, the air of bafflement in even such a home of rugby as Coventry, when the Cornish hordes descended upon it for a county final. The black and gold led to the general impression that Wolverhampton Wanderers were in town, and one astute favour-seller dug out some old Wolves cup final rosettes, so that many an innocent Cornishman cheered on his side while sporting a tin replica of the F.A. Cup.[1] 'Trelawney' was sung in the Broadgate, and when Sam Hooper, the Cornish R.F.U. treasurer, solemn as an old owl, announced that the Bishop of Truro would be holding a special

1. I must not, however, give the impression that a Cornish rugby crowd resembles soccer hooligans. The reasons for this difference are complex and more to do with Cornish virtues than any inherent merit in following rugby.

service of intercession beforehand in the new Coventry cathedral, he was widely believed. Many Cornishmen have told me that they knew other Cornishmen who went along to attend this mythical service.[1]

The Cornish devotion to rugby, I would guess, originates in their ancient sport of hurling, of which a relic survives at St Columb. In Cornish hurling (unlike Irish hurling, which is played with sticks) the object was to take the ball in the hands and run with it, just as William Webb Ellis is so dubiously said to have done, and place it in the goal, which was probably the churchyard of the next parish. The foundation of the game was the scrimmage. Thus the two essential elements were there, scrimmaging for the ball, and running with it, long before rugby was formalized. When the Rugby Football Union was formed little adjustment was needed. There had already been attempts to replace the old all-join-in hurling with more regular versions, and the change from the old game to the new was gradual, and in some cases scarcely noticed. The long Cornish wrestling tradition must also have helped.

Cornwall have, as I write, only won the county championship once, in 1908, when they went on to represent Britain in the Olympic Games. This was an odd little corner of history. Only twice has rugby been an Olympic sport: the second time was 1924, in Paris, and the winners were the United States (represented by Stanford University), who beat France in the final. No British team competed, and as Stanford were beaten by both Blackheath and the Harlequins on their way to France the standard was not high. In 1908, when the Games were held in London, Australia entered – they were

1. There was some disappointment felt with the Sutherland tapestry. Familiar with the work of Barbara Hepworth, the Cornish thought it tame and conventional.

over here on tour anyway; and Britain entered, presumably so that someone could give the Australians a game. But Britain did not take it too seriously, and chose the current county champions *en bloc* as their representatives. Australia beat Cornwall 32–3, and there were no other entries. Fifteen silver medals must still be knocking around somewhere in Cornwall.

Since those days Cornwall have often been strong challengers for the championship, and it is surprising they have not done better. Of course Cornwall has only a small population, but the number of fine players it has produced, and the vigour of their support, might have been expected to do more. In 1969 they played Lancashire at Redruth in the final, led by nine points at half-time, but still narrowly lost. Not only was every sitting and standing space on the Redruth ground occupied, but every neighbouring rooftop, every tree. When Cornwall had lost, the crowd, after giving both sides proper applause, walked away quietly. Their disappointment was deep – some of them had been waiting sixty years for the day – but there was no bitterness. They knew the rugby game, and realized how well Lancashire had played in the second half.

Cornwall's contribution to rugby is much greater than the number of matches it has won. The county championship is an odd, lop-sided affair (though I find it an attractive one, and doubt if any of the much-discussed new systems will improve it). In some areas the early matches are played in mid-week, before the merest scattering of spectators. Some players consider their clubs to be more important than their counties, and maybe only turn out for the county at all because it gives them a better chance of catching the eye of an international selector. Cornwall, more than anyone else, have imbued the championship with competitive enthusiasm, fired it with their own heat. After those three hectic semi-finals in 1967 the

Surrey players, I would wager, were more conscious of representing Surrey, more conscious of the concept of Surrey-hood, or however one likes to put it, than ever before. The same was true even of Warwickshire at Coventry, and the Lancastrians at Redruth. There is a stirring moment in *The Napoleon of Notting Hill*, where Adam Wayne, leading his municipal forces against the embattled armies of all the Kensingtons and their allies, cries out unceasingly, 'Notting Hill! Notting Hill!': until one of the opposing host is moved irritably to reply, 'Well, what about Bayswater?'

> 'We have won!' cried Wayne, striking his flagstaff in the ground. 'Bayswater for ever! We have taught our enemies patriotism!'

This might be a parable of Cornish rugby.

From Cornish rugby to Cornish Nonconformity is an easy transition, as we always say when there is no obvious connection between one subject and the next. At least, both are inspired by an evangelical fervour. Nonconformity in Cornwall principally means Methodism, and is not the force it was, but it has stamped itself into the Cornish character and will be there for centuries yet. I was much influenced by Cornish Nonconformity. It can be perverse and sometimes alarming, but I would not dream of condemning it.

I am thinking not so much of the relatively dignified Wesleyans, but some of their fiercer brethren. Take, for instance, that formidable denomination, the Bible Christians, fishermen and farmers and miners and (sometimes) profound biblical scholars. The Bible Christians were founded, somewhat inadvertently, early in the nineteenth century by William O'Bryan. For a long time they were colloquially known as 'Bryanites'. In 1907 they became part of the United Methodist Church, which in 1932 became part of the

Methodist Church, which will before too long, in the providence of God, become again part of the Church of England. But though it is more than sixty years since the Bible Christians had any separate denominational existence there are still people in Devon and Cornwall who call themselves Bible Christians, still chapels who insist on putting the name on their notice boards and posters for special occasions, in large letters even if in brackets. ('Ain't nuth'n like a Bible Christian 'arrvest.')

The Bible Christians were very much a Devon and Cornwall denomination, their home always in the south-west, but in ninety years after their foundation more than a thousand chapels were opened in ten different countries. The emigration of the miners, as tin came on hard times, no doubt helped; but it could not have been done without a fierce missionary drive.

The first chapel, forty feet by twenty, was opened at Shebbear in 1818, William O'Bryan preaching. He took as his text, 'Then Samuel took a stone and set it between Mizpeh and Shen, and called the name of it Ebenezer, saying, hitherto hath the Lord helped us.' Prayers were led by Mrs O'Bryan and another woman called Patience Bickle. In the evening, a young man called James Thorne, who was to become one of the heroes of the Bible Christians, took as his text, 'But we preach Christ crucified.' F. W. Bourne, the denomination's historian, says: 'It was a season to be remembered; great numbers were in distress, several found peace, and some were enabled to believe that the blood of Christ cleanseth from all sin.'[1]

I do not put these details in this book as an occasional piece of Nonconformist history which happens to have come my

1. *The Bible Christians: their Origin and History*. F. W. Bourne. The Bible Christian Book Room, 1905.

way. This was the background of much of my own experience. To those who have shared this experience such accounts are commonplace; to those who have not they are distasteful and sometimes hardly conceivable. What strikes us about it? The morning text indicates, one of many things which the Methodists shared with the old Dissenters, a passion for the place names of Israel. The Evangelical Revival brought with it a revival in the habit of bestowing on children some of the obscurer Biblical names, and even christening them with pious utterances and texts. 'Hallelujah' came into fashion again, though I know of no case comparable with the unfortunate seventeenth-century child who was named 'Bind-their-kings-with-chains-and-their-nobles-with-links-of-iron'.

Yet its climax – 'hitherto hath the Lord helped us' – has that defiant lift of the chin which made these people, often persecuted and often poor, such redoubtable crusaders. The evening text indicates, what was always to be true, that 'The Cross' was the centre of their faith: the unique, cosmic, personal, comprehensive act of God. The part played by women is notable: Nonconformists have always stressed the ministry of women. Not much wrong so far. But what of the 'scenes of distress' which accompanied conversion?

Scenes of distress did, and do often accompany evangelical conversions. They had been an accompaniment to the preaching of John Wesley, whose style depended more upon logic than emotion. A few years before O'Bryan preached at Shebbear, Hugh Bourne and William Clowes and their followers had been preaching in the midlands, at Mow Cop. These were big camp-meetings, already known as 'American-style', and at one of them 'four preachers were crying to sinners to flee from the wrath to come, and dealing out their lives at every stroke.'[1] These meetings led to the formation of the Primitive Methodist church, which flourished and spread from its midland base much as the Bible Christians had done in the west. William Clowes, a literate man, tried to describe his experience of conversion: 'What is this? . . . This is what Methodists mean by being converted. Yes, that is it – God is converting my soul. In an agony of prayer I believed God *would* save me, then I believed he *was* saving me, then I believed he *had* saved me. And it was so.' It is a retrospective account, and does not tell the outsider much, but we need not doubt the agony.

The truth is that Dissent has constantly fallen into the temptation of relishing the agony of conversion. I often have heard it argued that there can be no true conversion without distress. It does not follow, however, that the distress must be outwardly and visibly demonstrated. It does not follow that the more hysterical the occasion the surer the proof of God's hand. It is sound doctrine that men often find salvation through suffering. It does not follow that suffering is pleasing in the sight of God, and this I take to be the principal heresy which has afflicted Dissenting churches (though to be sure it is not theirs alone).

Edmund Warne, a friend and colleague of O'Bryan, wrote to his wife:

'There were many precious souls weeping around me, with

Tears which spake their sins forgiven
And sighs which waft the soul to heaven.

. . . Sinners are convinced, backsliders are coming back, with weeping and lamentations, believers are established in the faith,

1. A detailed account of the Mow Cop meetings, which were remarkable, is to be found in *Origin and History of the Primitive Methodist Church*, by H. B. Kendall.

and such powerful effects are produced by faith and prayer as I never before witnessed.'

Here is F. W. Bourne's account of a meeting conducted by Abraham Bastard. Abraham was an interesting character who had been a wrestler, in the savage Devon style, based on a kick to the legs with a heavy boot, not the relatively classical Cornish style. Then, in one of the peculiar traditions of the ring, he became a local preacher, and stayed one for half a century without backsliding. He was speaking at Treligga, and

> Half a score of persons at one time fell on their knees crying for mercy, several of them almost immediately receiving an answer of peace. The noise of some praising God aloud, and of others wrestling for salvation, could be heard afar. The meeting continued until a late hour. After it had been closed, a piercing voice was heard outside, and after a light had been procured, the preacher and others following the sound, discovered in an old lumber chamber a servant of the family on his knees, agonizing for salvation.

Another of the Bible Christian preachers, William Mason, visited a man supposed to be possessed of a devil.

> The wife and children left the house, and he was shut up with him a whole day. The first visit produced no visible good effects, nor did a second nor third, and he had to be bound with cords when the preacher left. On his last visit he spent a whole night with him, and had still a harder struggle. In the morning the man fell into such an agony that the perspiration arose from him like a cloud of steam from a fiercely boiling pot. His countenance gathered blackness, and bore a horrible inhuman appearance. He sank at last into a state of profound insensibility, followed by the help-

lessness of a child. From that time he became a changed man, and afterwards met in class.[1] He had been a powerful man physically, but he never recovered his strength, and was found dead one morning on his knees by the side of his bed.

This is a horrible little story, however you look at it. But it bears a recognizable relationship to some of the cautionary tales of my own childhood. There is another story, almost as bad, about a Primitive Methodist preacher called John Oxtoby. He was known as 'Praying Johnny', because he spent six hours of the day on his knees. He once went on a mission to Filey, and when he came in sight of the town he fell on his knees and prayed, until he had God's assurance of the success of his mission. When the assurance was granted he rose and rushed towards the town, crying 'Filey is taken! Filey is taken!' It was a very successful mission. He was asked by a fellow-preacher, who prayed less but read more, why the results of their preaching were so different, and Oxtoby replied, 'Oh, thou leads 'em to the tree o' knowledge, and I leads 'em to the tree o' life.'

However, this belief in the invincible merits of ignorance was not characteristic of the Primitive Methodists, nor the Bible Christians, nor of Nonconformity in general. They have always believed in education, even in education for the poor. Well they might, since they were convinced that education could only prove the validity of their beliefs. This has not always turned out to be the case: increasingly the education and the agony have seemed to be saying different things. But to this day Dissent has never become Oxtobic: has never doubted that there is only one tree, that knowledge and life

1. *class:* the Methodist class-meeting, usually midweek meetings for prayer and Bible study.

are the fruits of the same root. I write of orthodox Dissent, what today would be described as 'mainstream' Dissent. Every generation has its Fifth Monarchists, as it has its Inquisition, and in turbulent times any authority, however irrational, has an appeal if it is authoritative enough. Men prefer peace of mind to knowledge, which I suppose is why Jesus, even though he preached peace, said that he had come to bring a sword.

So most of the nineteenth-century local preachers, as well as ministers, made desperate efforts to 'give their sons an education', and many of the sons benefited from it in one way or another, though they did not always become preachers. Sometimes they went to parliament instead.

Billy Bray never went to parliament, though many worse men and worse speakers did. Billy was a Cornish Bible Christian. He learned, after much struggling, to read and write, and even left a rough autobiography. It has never been published, although F. W. Bourne's short life of him, *Billy Bray, the King's Son* (Epworth Press), while in some ways superficial, is a moving account. Billy was a tin miner who, after he was converted, became the best known and best loved of Cornish local preachers. 'Come, all of 'ee,' he would cry, 'ragged arse or no, feyther do truly love 'ee.' He was always generous and always poor. He used to say, 'Feyther will provide, if 'tis what feyther do want,' and he found that he and 'feyther' were usually of one mind. Billy built chapels with his own hands, begging the money and materials as he went along. Several of the preachers did this: wanderers themselves, travelling on foot, often hungry and weary, often mocked – but determined that, where they had passed, the Word should have a local habitation and a name.

The name, now that was important. Ugly, square little buildings those chapels seem to us, such as have survived, but what names they had! *Siloam*, whither men come blind and depart seeing. *Bethesda*, the house of mercy. *Rehoboth*, 'for the Lord hath made a rock for us.' *Salem*, for the peace of God has been there. *Great Deliverance*: that was one of Billy Bray's chapels. What church anywhere has had a better name than that? What are Notre Dame and St Paul's besides *Great Deliverance*? What kind of experience makes a man build a chapel with his own hands and give it such a name? Something more, I think, than fits of hysteria. Nor will anyone who lacks an ear for the ring of that phrase ever understand the forces that have moved English Dissent, and helped to shape the character of England, which for this purpose we may take to include Cornwall. It may be that the Puritans' suspicion of some of the other arts gave them a heightened feeling for noble and vivid language, as a blind man is said to acquire especially sensitive hearing. William Tyndale, John Milton, Billy Bray: even the awful Oxtoby could not help hitting off a fine phrase.

And still with the agony and the earnestness there went the humour, the laughing, which is never better illustrated than in the tales of Cornish preachers, sometimes I dare say contrived for a laugh in the first place, certainly constantly repeated by themselves to themselves. They often drew their illustrations from mining. 'Ta-ake pile o' best ore,' said one, and then, peering over the pulpit, 'like Cap'n[1] 'Ancock down there do know all about . . .' There was the announcement of a forthcoming special united service: 'Addresses will be given by Salvation Army major and Baptist minister – and I tell 'ee when Salvation fire and Baptist water do get together, tedden long afore steam's up!' They were not above giving God a bit of advice or information. 'Looard, as thou wilt ha' seen in today's *West Briton* . . .' And at the time of the Armenian

1. Mine-captain.

atrocities: 'Feyther, if I were thee for five minutes, I'd blow all they Turks to smithereens.' And at prayer meeting, one to another: 'No need to shout, brother. Feyther idden deaf.'

'There stood the preacher,' wrote George Borrow in *Lavengro*, 'one of those men – and thank God their number is not few – who, animated by the Spirit of Christ, amidst much poverty, and, alas, much contempt, persist in carrying the light of the Gospel amidst the dark parishes of what, but for their instrumentality, would scarcely be Christian England.'

Because their cries seem strange to us they were not necessarily unheard. No doubt we shall seem to our descendants primitive, foolish and inarticulate men. But feyther idden deaf. This was the discovery of Christ, the Christian consolation.

The strength of Nonconformity in Cornwall has helped the Liberal party to survive there, even through the hardest times. Only one Liberal deposit has ever been lost in Cornwall. That was in the Falmouth/Camborne division in 1951. The circumstances were unfortunate, although the candidate was a trier. In 1955 the seat was not contested, and this was the only occasion in this century when the Liberals have not fought a Cornish division. This unsatisfactory state of affairs was remedied by a group of enthusiastic people, some of them in the traditional Methodist pattern, some new not only to Liberalism but to politics, who nevertheless worked happily together, who put the association on a sound footing, and invited me to become their president. In due course I became the prospective candidate, and fought the 1959 election. We did not set the Fal on fire, but nearly doubled the 1951 vote, almost reaching 8000, over twenty per cent, which was better than we expected. It was an interesting experience from which I learned much, and I look back on it with pleasure. It brought me many friendships.

At first I intended to stand for the division again, and was re-adopted. But my life at this time was hectic, involving much travelling and many professional engagements at short notice. I would set aside an evening for a meeting in Cornwall, and then be asked to give a broadcast in – it might be – Newcastle. I was making a fair living but was hardly in a position to turn down work often. The Falmouth/Camborne Liberals, after their efforts, were entitled to a candidate who could give them more time, more regularly. At the same time I had become active in the Liberal affairs of Plymouth.

Liberalism in Plymouth was not quite dead, but had scarcely given a twitch for years. Then my wife fought a by-election in the Peverell ward, and caused a stir by coming second, above the Labour candidate. The Labour candidate was an old friend, Reg Scott, then the West Country correspondent of the *Daily Mirror*. The Conservative candidate, Frank Prout, was another old friend, who had been a member of my father's church at Totnes. So it was a matey election, but nevertheless a break-through for the Liberals, for this was some time before Orpington man made his dramatic (and in some ways enduring) appearance. At the next municipal elections in Plymouth we fought six wards, won none, but took three second places and did badly nowhere. Those elections were fought with a paid-up membership, in the two Plymouth divisions, of less than seventy. The organization had to be centralized, and was chiefly carried out from my office (one room), under the auspices of my secretary, Elfrieda. Elfrieda was a tall, dark girl; good-looking in the way one would call willowy; charming and efficient, but not at all the general idea of a political manager. I doubt if she had any profound Liberal convictions. Yet she handled those elections like a veteran, and had she chosen, might ultimately, so I will always think, have made a national agent for the Liberals or anyone else.

As a result of these developments it seemed a good idea to switch my parliamentary candidature from Falmouth to the Sutton division of Plymouth. I thought I might meet the responsibilities better if I was nearer my base. With the agreement of all concerned, this was done. The next year we again fought six wards in Plymouth, won two, and in the wards we fought actually polled more votes than either of the other parties. This seemed at the time a great achievement, and still seems so to me in retrospect. We had by now hundreds and hundreds of members, the majority of them young, keen, bright. It was a blow when soon afterwards I was asked to resign my candidature. I was succeeded as parliamentary candidate by the chairman of the meeting which had asked me to resign. After a short period he joined the Labour party, leaving the Plymouth Liberals in disarray.

Nevertheless it was a correct decision to ask me to resign, if not taken for the correct reasons. I was not well, physically or mentally, and the breakdown of my marriage was near. The fault for this was much more mine that my wife's, but not entirely mine. She had led the Liberals in Plymouth through two municipal elections, and if she had scrambled the extra few votes needed to win her seat on the last occasion many things for Liberalism in that city would have been different. As it was, she resigned when I did, not from love, perhaps, but loyalty. She is still an active Liberal, as I am myself, if not quite with the intensity of those days: I look back with warmth upon our political associations. In these at least we never differed.

This has taken me over the border from Cornwall, but rounds off the political part of the story. Those years as the candidate for Falmouth enhanced my love for Cornwall, and also gave me some insight into its economic dilemma. I see from a recent (1974) survey that seventy-four per cent of Cornishmen think that the county gets too many visitors, and eighty-four per cent think that the tourist board should stop trying to attract them. Furthermore, seventy-three per cent would like to limit the number of visitors, even if it meant setting up checkpoints on the boundary. And given the proposition that increasing tourism 'would not harm the beauty of Cornwall too much', ninety-one per cent disagreed with it.

I treat these figures with some caution, but am not altogether surprised by them. A summer's day in the narrow streets of what was once a pretty little fishing village, now crammed to bursting with tourists and their cars, can be a harrowing experience. For three months of the year the natives effectively lose their own towns, submerged fathoms deep by the touring tide, as the lost land of Lyonnesse was drowned by the sea. I know of several people who retired to places on the Cornish coast, and left again because they could not stand the summers.

But there is more to it than discomfort and any spoiling of the landscape. It is at root a matter of pride. Cornishmen are warm-hearted, but fiercely independent, sometimes xenophobic. Looking after tourists is not the way of life they would naturally relish. But the tin and copper mines are almost all gone. Only the derelict stacks remain, with their resounding names – Penandrea, Wheal Grambler, Ding Dong, Honey and Trelawney, Wheal Bloody Nose – telling of a vanished prosperity. There is a good deal of sentimental thinking about the mines – it was a rough life, and when attempts have been made to reopen one or two Cornishmen have not rushed to go down – but it was more of a man's life than selling ice-cream for half the year. The great days of Cornish fishing have gone. The huer's house still stands on the cliff at St Ives, but no longer does the cry go up from it when the schools of pilchard are sighted in the bay. The pilchard, they will say sadly, is a wayward fish. The only fishing boats you are likely to see at St Ives now are a few French crabbers. It is better in some other places, but if Cornish fishing villages actually had to depend on fishing they would mostly have a thin time of it.

There is china clay in the east of the county, there is engineering at Camborne, there are docks at Falmouth, there is an assortment of light industry, but Cornwall has become heavily dependent on tourism, and is unhappy about it. It is not the tourists that are disliked, but the dependence. More should be done, it is felt, to attract to the county light industry which would not be subject to a seasonal trade; but tourism brings with it about seventy-five million pounds a year, and it would take a lot of light industry to replace that.

It is an old question. In the 1890s Sir Arthur Quiller-Couch founded the *Cornish Magazine*, and the early issues were full of it. Generally the idea of tourists was welcomed, but there was no recognition of what would be involved. Sir Joseph Fayrer, Bart, pointed out that 'the scenery is charming; the objects of antiquarian and historical interest are numerous; there are the usual opportunities of shooting and bathing', and clearly thought that ought to be enough for anybody. Sir Edward Durning-Lawrence, MP, declared that Cornwall must be 'discovered', and suggested promenades, military bands, open-air cafés. This provoked wrathful replies. Mr J. L. W. Page begged 'for goodness' sake let us have some place that knows not the tripper'. There was a curious letter from the Penzance Medical Officer of Health. 'Above all,' he said, speaking of the tourists, 'I would plead for their possible infirmities of digestion. I have known visitors . . . driven from the field, vanquished in a brave and pitiful struggle with food comforts readily assimilated by our robuster selves.' Four knife and fork meals a day, I suppose, and every one of them a pasty.[1]

Q himself summed up the discussion. Because of the county's economic depression, he saw no alternative to tourist development. 'Since we must cater for the stranger,' he wrote, 'let us do it well and honestly. Let us respect him *and* our native land.' He was dubious about promenades and bands, but said: 'I have dreamed . . . of a broad and noble coast road: but always I awoke, and lo, it was a dream.' The fastest form of road transport known to Q then was the push-bike. Soon they will be coming down a broad motorway to Cornwall, more and more of them, for better or worse: and I doubt if a picket line across Bodmin Moor – which has recently been suggested by some militant Cornishmen – can stop them.

There has always been some argument as to which is the county town of Cornwall, so it may be as well if I give the authoritative answer, as follows: *Bodmin is, Launceston used to be, Truro ought to be, and Penryn thinks it is.* Denys Val Baker, in an amusing radio programme ('Cornwall for the Cornish') described how Cornwall seized independence. They fought a

1. The Cornish pasty has changed its nature since the mines decayed. The point about a Cornish pasty used to be that the pastry was hard, so that it could be slipped into a miner's pocket without being damaged. There is a story about a Cornishman who, on a visit to London, met a girl who was a cook, and subsequently married her. She was particularly proud of her light, flaky pastry. On the first day after the honeymoon she gave him his pasty as he set off to the mine. She waited in the evening for a commendation, but he was silent on the subject. After a week she asked him whether anything was wrong with her pasties. 'Naw, naw,' he said. ' 'Tis just this m'dear – well, what us do call a pasty, 'tis like the ones Jan Pascoe's wife do make – why, t'other day he dropped one down shaft and when us got to bottom 'twas all in one piece.' It is also widely held that the devil never visits Cornwall, because he is scared that as soon as he crossed the Tamar he would be seized by a housewife and clapped in a pasty. This suggests that there was no particularity as to a pasty's contents!

successful war against the English, but the constitutional formalities were delayed, because nobody could agree where the Cornish capital should be. They were forced to conduct the negotiations from the temporary capital, a boat in Falmouth harbour. It all ended happily with the signing of a peace treaty on the Tamar Bridge, and a generous speech by the English Prime Minister (you could not tell whether it was John Snagge imitating Harold MacMillan, or Harold Macmillan imitating John Snagge).

I sometimes think that the Cornish problem is epitomized, or at least exemplified, in the experience of Derek and Jeannie Tangye. They made a heartfelt, utterly determined decision to break away from the pressures of London life (though they had both been highly successful in their about-town careers) and went to live at Dorminack, a then derelict cottage on the Cornish cliffs, near Lamorna. Derek had been a journalist, who reached the eminence of telling the *Express* he did not want to be William Hickey, and Jeannie had been the public relations officer for the Savoy group of hotels. They were giving up a great deal, almost everything, by the standards of the world which they were leaving. They started a flower and vegetable farm. They had terrible troubles. With courage that can scarcely be comprehended, even when you have seen the terrain in winter, they stuck it out. All the friends who had confidently prophesied, 'See you back in six months,' were confounded. They were out of the rat-race (the phrase was then becoming fashionable). They were entirely occupied, mentally and physically, almost broke; and at peace. They had, needless to say, no television; no telephone, even. It was a mile and a half of rutted lane to the nearest road, and another mile to the nearest village, St Buryan. I know all this to be true for in those days I knew them well.

Then Derek wrote the story of their adventures, *A Gull on*

the Roof. Years later I read it, at his request, in 'Storytime' on Radio 4, and still found it moving. He wrote it simply, unaffectedly, unboastfully. It was a true account. It was an immediate, thundering best seller. Publishers and public demanded more. Why not? With the profits the Tangyes could buy proper greenhouses, have running water and electricity, turn a chicken coop into a spare room, get some kitchen equipment for Jeannie to bake her bread, employ assistants on the farm. Why not? So the books were written. Derek wrote a series of successors to *A Gull on the Roof*, which continues equally successfully. Jeannie wrote *Meet Me at the Savoy*, and a novel on the same theme, *Hotel Regina* ('a bit saucy in parts,' said Derek when he read it, a shade thoughtfully).

I wrote in a review of one of Derek's books: 'There is some confusion about the Tangye books, even among those who have read them. They have charm, of course: but they are also, quite seriously, social documents. The Tangyes have reacted to the human situation as decisively as, say, Daniel Cohn-Bendit, though in a different direction. They have found their philosophy, however unfashionable, and live it.'

Well, so they did, so they do – or at least they try. Minack is still there. The farm is a genuine farm, and flourishes. They still work at it themselves, though they can now afford to have helpers, and do. There is still no telephone. There is a television set, but it is kept in a cupboard. The bread is still home-baked. The road is still rutted. What has changed?

They did not go to Minack to write. The books were initially no more than by-products. All the same they have ceased to be flower farmers, primarily, and become celebrities. People travel from all over Britain, and from many other countries, to see them. The Tangyes receive their hundreds of visitors every year, if not always with enthusiasm, with courtesy. They take the view that if these people have read the books, and are sufficiently interested to come to see for themselves, they should not be spurned. This is unquestionably right; but it has changed the situation of the Tangyes, and perhaps their characters a little. They fled London because they hated fame, and now they are famous again. I am not suggesting that their efforts have been in any way unworthy, or lost. They have the beauty of Minack always with them, and not many visitors make the journey during the winter storms. But they have achieved no more than a partial escape, just as Cornwall itself has achieved no more than a partial escape. Perhaps partial escapes are the best anyone can hope for.

The Cornish coast, of which the Minack cliffs are a good example, is nearly all beautiful – at its wildest as noble as anything Devon has, at its gentlest as warming. There is something in the light, the colours, which makes the Cornish coastal villages especially lovely. I am told that this cannot really be so, that it is nothing but a long-standing myth which makes artists flock to St Ives, but I reject the rational view. Never have I seen such translucency of sky and sea, of spring and autumn colours at dawn and dusk, as looking across St Ives Bay. Porthcurnow is almost as good. Every day is different, and every different day is different again from the same day anywhere else. I am subject, you see, to the traditional illusion. But even if beauty is only in the eye of the beholder it is splendid to be the beholder.

Cornwall inland is marred by the mines. Less because they are ugly – the impression they give, as the ivy grows on the stacks, is sometimes romantic rather than uncouth – but because it is hard to look upon them without sadness. I have said that I do not believe tin mining has a serious future in Cornwall, but this does not mean that I relish the decay of the industry, any more than I relish the departure of the Bible

Christians, and the sight of so many Methodist chapels turned into cinemas, or warehouses, or left desolate in the countryside.

Towards the end of the nineteenth century a Cornish couple, Mr and Mrs Pryor, emigrated and settled at Moonta, in South Australia. Their son Oswald was born at Moonta, began work in the mines there at the age of thirteen, and eventually became surface manager, a position he held for ten years. In his spare time he drew cartoons, which capture the atmosphere of the Cornwall that is past and passing. A collection of Oswald Pryor's cartoons was published over here by the London Cornish Association under the title *A Cornish Pasty*. He also wrote a book on the subject, *Australia's Little Cornwall*, (Angus & Robertson, 1963). The Cornish community in South Australia remained close-knit and largely self-contained. They created a miniature replica of the life of their homeland, which survived longer than in many places the original did. We see the choir-master leading the practice: *Come on boays, double effs, guv-un-guts!* And the local preacher: *We thank thee, Lord, for what little spark o' grace we do possess. O Lord, water that spark!* There was a chapel orchestra in one Australian town, with no less than seven bassoons, and *when they all closed down on low F, 'twas like 'eaven.* All these things, you would say at once, are Tuckingmill or Praze-an-Beeble? No, they are the Moonta district of South Australia, but it is all the same, for Cornwall lives wherever there is a Cornishman. Mind, the Australians enjoyed a trip home:

> ''Ow did 'ee enjoy your trip back Cornwall, Maister Treloar?'
> 'Splendid, John. I sing'd to fower funerals.'

I have two favourites among Mr Pryor's cartoons. There is the chapel concert, the piano with the candlesticks and aspidistra, the fancy hats in the front row, the next performers peeping round the stage curtains, and the MC, commanding and jovial, announcing '*My dotter will now sing, ''Alice, whur be gwan to''*.' And the last of all in his book: there is the mine in the background, at night, with a slightly derelict, Heath Robinson air to it – and there is Cousin Jack, doing nicely thank you, stepping it out erratically for home. A goat peers at him over the fence. He lifts his hat solemnly. 'Goo'night, cap'n,' he says politely, and steps into a pond. Thus an age ended. 'Goo'night, cap'n,' into the pond, and the mine is alone, deserted and crumbling.

13 Moorhaven

In the autumn of 1963 I entered Moorhaven Psychiatric Hospital, near Ivybridge, as a voluntary patient. I stayed for a few days, did not like it much, and left. This was a mistake. A few weeks later I was sent back there compulsorily, and stayed for some months. This happened amid much publicity – at least in local terms – as I had tried to kill myself, and almost succeeded. I had also been arrested for being unfit to drive through drink and drugs, and had had a set-to with the police. These last happenings were, however, by-products of my misery, not its cause.

This was all very horrible, and must have been perplexing to those who knew me only as a face on the screen or a voice on the air: surely a successful and popular man? I am not sure of the causes. My marriage was breaking down. No doubt I overworked, and drank too much. For a long time I had been unable to sleep without a very large dose of barbiturate. But when all these and other things have been considered, there was something irrational about it, and this 'something', I suppose, this irrational residuum, is mental illness. I cannot see, looking back, any adequate reason why the world became so utterly black, and remained so, with some intermissions, for a long time.

I often think of a passage in the autobiography of R. C. Robertson-Glasgow, a man whom, to my deep regret, I never knew. He was a man of many talents, apart from being one of the best of cricket writers. He wrote: '. . . only those who have suffered it know the hell of nervous illness. Twice again was I to be similarly afflicted. This much of good has emerged from it all: first, that I have learnt to regard physical ailments with the contempt that nine-tenths of them deserve; and secondly, that I know the unutterable delight of health found after a long and seemingly hopeless search.'[1] I cannot go so far as that, but it is an encouraging thought. His book, which is full of gaiety, comradeship and wit, ends with the thought that we learn by suffering, and a toast to 'tomorrow'. He was then forty-six. He killed himself seventeen years later. I have been told that his house in the country was surrounded by snow, which he found acutely depressing. He took an overdose. The ambulance was sent for. The snow prevented it arriving in time. So the black dog got him in the end.

And yet when one considers all that Robertson-Glasgow did in those sixty-three years, and the constant stream of affectionate reminiscence that flows from his friends whenever his name is mentioned, it is hard to believe that he really lost the battle. This too is a comforting thought to those similarly afflicted. I say 'similarly', but of course no two cases are identical, and my neuroses are not those of Robertson-Glasgow. Nor have I responded with the same courage. As far as physical affliction goes, when a couple of years later I had another long spell in hospital with neuritis in my leg the pain was so acute that I remember praying wryly, 'O Lord please take it away and give me back my neuroses.' But Robertson-Glasgow is right, and it is after all a scriptural doctrine, and I keep coming back to it as to a talisman, that we learn by suffering. I am a better man now than I was before I went to Moorhaven. Not much, perhaps: but better.

I shall never be completely free from irrational mental stresses. I know I shall continue, from time to time, to have fits of dark depression and bitter temper. But I am, I think, learning to control them a little, and mitigate their effects. It

1. *46 Not Out*, by R. C. Robertson-Glasgow. Hollis & Carter, 1949.

requires a conscious readjustment of one's approach to life. In my case it has meant, among other things, being a good deal less ambitious, and this is certainly beneficial, if only because it is easier not to be envious. If you have a car which is liable to miss on a cylinder (I hope I have the mechanical metaphor right) you do not enter it for the Monte Carlo rally. But there is just as much satisfaction to be got from coaxing it safely through the Cotswolds.

However, it is not my purpose to give my own medical history, nor am I qualified to give instruction in the principles of psychiatry. What might be helpful is some comment on what it feels like to be a mental patient, or rather (since there are such wide varieties of mental illness) what it is like to be inside a mental hospital. The difficulty is that, while inside, one's thoughts by the nature of things are rarely coherent; and when one is out, relief blurs the edges of memory, even tints the clouds pink. Spasmodically, in Moorhaven, I kept a diary, for the only time in my life. I find it mostly trivial and self-pitying: all the time I am trying to reassure myself that I am not really mad. Nevertheless, I subjoin a few extracts, as they are likely to give a more accurate impression of what went on in my mind than a retrospect twelve years later. I have changed the names of the patients. The extracts begin when I had been there only a week or two.

13 December In the little lounge a radio soprano is singing (rather well) 'The Last Rose of Summer'. After a tremendous shouting fit Leslie has settled down. The nurse has left him and gone into the dormitory to see Jack, who is quiet too – has been all day, except for a bad spell this morning, and again, about an hour ago, when a new arrival came in. Leslie and Jack always – consciously? – put on a big show for new arrivals. For a few minutes it might almost be a normal hospital ward. The Bull walks through from the lounge, scowling. This morning we had a great scene when he thought a pound had been stolen from his locker. It was in his pocket. This evening we had another scene when he announced a half-crown had been stolen. Diligent search, checking of his resources and spending, and sure enough half a crown is missing. Psychiatrist Gibson deduces that he has hidden it, so that by scene 2 he may justify his humiliation in scene 1. Consciously? What does 'consciously' mean in this context anyway? Leslie gets a telephone message to say his mother is coming to see him tomorrow. This starts him off: a scream, a sob, a scream again. 'Mother, father, Michael, I'm here, this is your son, Leslie, your son.' The new arrival is in bed, just his face showing. He is a chubby man with a round, pink, scared face. He has not said a word to anybody since he came in, but as I look at him a large round tear trickles down his cheek.

15 December A lot of heartening letters from friends and listeners, many quite unknown to me. I dare say there have been some rude ones, too, which have been tactfully sorted out. The last twenty-four hours have been dominated by the saga of Jack's petition. He lives in one of the little separate dormitories at the end of the ward. A very strange mixture indeed. Aged 30? 35? Bearded. Virtually illiterate; he can't read or spell, but can write out clumsy capital letters if you dictate them to him. He is slightly built but very strong. He has won a judo brown belt, which he keeps in his room, and the staff say he might even have won a black one had he been able to master the Japanese terms. Not unnaturally, they are a little cagey of him! For most of the time he is even-tempered, indeed gentle; he is very good, for instance, with young Leslie – and he is well enough liked in the hospital. But he can be very awkward and even, at times, savage. He has covered the walls of his room with paintings, mostly religious, including a rather good nativity and a horrible crucifixion which he calls 'abstract'. He has some sense of shape and colour, but can't draw. He has also inscribed various worthy mottoes, including

BE KIND TO EVERYONE
IT WILL MAKE YOU HAPPY

and erected what he calls his 'altar', a little table and a cloth with two flowers in pots (pinched from the main ward). It is his fourth time in here. They think he may be in this time for up to a year. Whether he can ever be cured must be very doubtful.

Well, Jack last night took a grudge against Mr Gomme, the senior charge nurse of the ward. Gomme is a capital fellow (he was not on duty at the time) but Jack had taken offence at some casual remark he had made. Last evening he emerged from his room with a document headed

A PETIEN AGISS GOM

and proceeded to ask all the patients, and indeed the staff too, for their signatures. It was suggested that the heading was hardly self-explanatory. So after taking infinite pains Jack added the words

FO HOPSULIN PETNS

('a petition against Gomme for upsetting the patients'). No one would sign, except the ancient Ceylonese, who is willing to sign anything in the hope that it will get him back to Ceylon. But Jack became increasingly pressing and increasingly fractious. He became quite threatening to poor Simon, who apparently also has had a spot of bother with Mr Gomme at one time. Simon, always highly nervous, was almost distracted between Jack's accusations that he was 'yellow' and the fear of doing anything, however trivial, which might jeopardize his hopes for an early discharge. The situation was saved by the nurse on duty, who finally offered to sign. He wrote down, beneath Jack's bold headings, the words

WE LIKE MR GOMME

and added his name. Half a dozen others promptly did the same, and Jack retired, proudly clutching the document which he believed would encompass the ruin of his foe.

We expected him to have forgotten all about it in the morning, but in fact there was a rather touching sequel. I had not signed the petition itself, even in its amended form, thinking it a little hard to exercise such a deception on such a person even if it kept him happy (or is my conscience becoming unnecessarily touchy in my present chastened condition?). First thing Jack was by my bed waving his piece of paper. He seemed quiet and good-tempered, and I pointed out, along with little Dai, the discrepancy between his big notice 'BE KIND TO EVERYONE' and his campaign against poor Mr Gomme. He went back to his room, and returned some minutes later. 'Right,' he announced. 'Not Crissen. Torn it up.' Then a pause. 'Still hate Mr Gomme. But torn it up. Not Crissen.' He went back to his room and slept nearly all day. I am an insufferable prig.

18 December Leslie is the kind of boy for whom one theoretically feels immense sympathy: but it would be much easier to feel if one did not have to share the same ward with him. He is sixteen, tall and thin, and I don't think he can ever have been a very prepossessing child, but it is difficult to be sure of that, because last October he received some very severe head injuries in a motor cycle accident, and now that the general hospital has put the physical damage right as best they can, Moorhaven tackles the more difficult task of repairing his mind.

The accident's effect on Leslie seems to have been to 'knock the cover off' his mind. All the simple longings and fears, which we all suffer but which we usually contrive more or less to conceal, are exposed. Thus all of us here must at times have murmured the name of a loved one whom we are missing. Leslie screams the names at the top of his voice for hours on end. 'Mother – father – mummy – daddy – come quickly! It's your son Leslie! Come quickly! I love my mother and father. I love you, mother and father. Mother! Father!' Then he announces that he is 'sick of this dump', and is going home, and he marches out of the ward and down the corridor, still hollering, till he reaches the partition, and the nurses – at whose patience I constantly marvel – gently lead him back.

But this simple principle, 'If you want something, yell for it,' operates at all levels of his mind. Sometimes unpleasantly: he is liable to go up to any woman in the ward with straightforward and crudely phrased suggestions. The other day my friend Bill – whom for some reason Leslie calls Tom – gave him a Mars bar. He is deeply devoted to Mars bars. He is now convinced that 'Tom' is an unending source of them, though in fact he had no more, and no means of obtaining any. For two hours the ward resounded with cries of 'Tom! Gimme Mars bar.' Then, *sotto voce*, 'Go on, Tom, go on. Just one Mars bar. Then I'll stop shouting.' Bill's kindly act did not make him popular. This morning we have had three days of continuous wailing, shrieking and groaning. The fact that it is tragic makes it none the less trying.

20 December Bill used to keep a pub. A friendly, inoffensive, very intelligent little man is Bill, and when he was behind his bar he courteously refused the drinks which his customers pressed on him. A lemonade was the most they could persuade him to take. But as soon as the pub was closed and he had cleared up carefully he would quietly go to his room and drink a bottle of brandy in a few large gulps. His liver is now in such a state that quite a small drink might easily kill him. So they sent him here. This morning he came back after a long session with his psychiatrist. He grinned at me, a little ruefully, and said: 'He's like a bloody kaolin plaster.' I asked why, and he said, 'He just draws everything out of you.'

21 December There was – or so it seemed to me – a richly comic moment at the Ward Meeting yesterday. The chairs were grouped more or less formally, with one set centrally and apart for the chairman. However, the doctor who runs the proceedings chose to sit away to one side, and the central chair was left vacant. Discussion proceeded in the usual desultory way. There wasn't much to liven things up, as Jack was asleep and Leslie wandering down the passage somewhere. We could hear his cries in the distance. The Bull was launched on a long dissertation on the advantages of providing the hospital with a stereophonic sound radio service. He is a great hi-fi man, and has worked out a scheme which would only cost a few thousand pounds (the hospital is already overspent on its patients' amenities fund). No one paid much attention, and he drifted into silence. In the pause which followed, Leslie entered. He marched, quite briskly, to the chairman's empty seat, sat down, glanced round. Every eye turned on him. He cleared his throat, leant forward, and spoke to us in a businesslike way, as if he were opening a board meeting. And what he said was, 'I love my mother and father. They give me Mars bars.' End of meeting.

After some time in this sick ward at Moorhaven, I was moved to the adjacent hospital, Moorfields, for patients who were not physically ill and not considered dangerous.

24 December This is very different from the reception block at Moorhaven. I have a room to myself, a pleasant view across the South Hams – I can just see the top of the tower of Ugborough church, in the next valley – a comfortable chair, and a table for work. It is quiet here, away from the main buildings. Most of the patients are old men, and they sit in the dayroom for hours on end, staring in front of them, scarcely saying a word. The only animation they show is after meals, when they can move quite smartly in their anxiety to dodge the washing-up. The few active ones don't really mind, as things get done more swiftly without the elders.

This morning, allowed out for a walk, I met an old man of eighty who has been in Moorhaven for fifty years. They say that the only thing that worries him is the thought that he might be declared sane and sent out. It is the kind of story one has heard before, but certainly he seemed cheerful and contented. I hoped for some interesting comments on the changes in the system during his time, but he would only say, 'Ah! Lots o' changes. Lots o' changes.'

So there have been, of course. Even fifteen years ago a

patient such as Jack would have been in a padded cell. Gomme came here in 1949, and remembers when they took the locks off the doors in the non-dangerous wards. The results were much as one would expect: a spate of getaways and then, when people had got used to the idea, fewer than before.

Although I am glad to have moved, in an odd way I miss the hurly-burly of the sick ward. I went down to see them and it was like meeting old friends. Jack has great plans for a special Christmas service at his altar. The Bull has been having electrical treatment and seems to be responding to it. At any rate he said 'Good morning' quite normally and cheerfully.

Christmas Day This is my second Christmas in hospital. The first was in 1944, in a military hospital, and I was contented enough then to stay unheroically in a nice warm comfortable bed. This time one's hopes and anxieties are all for getting out. Not that I am uncomfortable, but the longer one stays in here the bigger grow the problems (financial problems, for instance) that must be faced afterwards. Perhaps there was something in the point of view of the old chap who settled here for life.

Some have gone home for Christmas. I did not seek to, myself. Much better stay and waste no time in recovery. Considerable agony among patients who have been hoping they would be allowed home, if only for the day, and then been unlucky – or misbehaved. Exeats seem to be granted on grounds of good behaviour rather than improved health, but then I suppose here they amount to much the same thing.

I doubt whether hospitals have the right approach to Christmas. I have sometimes thought this in the past when

I have been visiting. For most of us Christmas is a festival of the home. Crackers and trees and preserved fruits and stockings and bright new pennies and all the rest lose most of their meaning when they are taken out of a family context.

In a mental hospital, anyway, the best thing to do with Christmas is to take as little notice of it as possible. There would be an outcry if this was the policy, and the patients would join in, partly on principle and partly because of a wish not to hurt the feelings of the staff. But in their hearts I do believe this is what most of the patients here feel. The reminders are too uncomfortable. The decorations and extra grub and sing-songs call up memories which are better kept in their place. I played some carols on the old piano in the dayroom last night, and by the third one everyone was crying. *Joy to the world, the Lord is come.*

From this point my diary becomes preoccupied with general and sententious reflections, but I will add one or two more recollections of this trying period of my life.

I remember the day when friendly little Bill, the secret brandy drinker, first came to the sick ward and was put in the bed opposite to me. He kept saying to himself – and only to himself, because nobody ever really listened to anyone but themselves in that ward – 'Didn't expect to finish up here. Didn't expect that. Knew I was taking a drop too much, but didn't think I was a nutcase. Didn't think I was a nutcase. Quite a surprise to me, that was.'

Before long – in four or five hours' time – the duty doctor would come round, and glance casually at the new admissions. I do not use 'casually' disdainfully. The duty doctor had a great many wards to cover, and if he let himself be anything but casual he would never have got round them. Bill's was the typical worry of the new patient, and it would receive the typical response: something like, 'Don't worry. This is just an ordinary hospital. You're sick, and we're going to make you well. We'll have you right pretty quickly.'

It seems sound therapy to insist on the idea of the 'ordinary hospital'. Moorhaven's approach was based on this principle, and I understand it is still common practice (what is more, Moorhaven has always been considered a very good hospital, and I do not doubt it for a moment).

An ordinary hospital. Sometimes the illusion is convincing. The wards look the same. There is the same smell, a mixture of disinfectant and linoleum and sweat. The custard is identical with that of every hospital in the land. There are, however, bound to be moments when the illusion breaks down, even in the calmer quarters. At lunch, once, I offered my neighbour the bread. He answered, politely, 'No thanks, I don't smoke.' This sounds funny in retrospect, but was not funny at the time. Had I, I worried, offered him a cigarette, and not the bread? And he, I dare say, was thinking – it *was* a cigarette he offered me, wasn't it? In five minutes we were both struggling with the familiar mental hospital situation: '*I* am sane enough – it's *he* who is dotty.' With every second of this thought we become increasingly doubtful of our own sanity. And all this was probably the result of a simple aural misunderstanding, of the kind which happens to us every day of our lives.

So, despite the routinely cheerful duty doctor, it cannot ever be quite *an ordinary hospital*. The doctors and nurses, who live most of their lives in surroundings which have become familiar, cannot easily comprehend the severity of the impact which mere admission to a mental hospital has on most people, as it did on little Bill, as it did on me, for all my attempts to be conscientiously articulate. To be there at all, this is the terrifying thing.

My experience of the weekly ward meetings was too limited for me to form any certain opinions about their value. They are well intended. The patients are invited to discuss with the staff, not their personal problems – though these keep breaking in – but the problems concerning the ward, the hospital as a whole. The nurses (usually male nurses in a men's ward) attend in mufti. At one meeting we were discussing the difficulties which mental patients find in obtaining employment when they leave hospital (Moorhaven had good connections with some helpful firms, but the difficulties are obvious enough). After a long and, as usual, rather aimless discussion, one man burst out: 'The trouble is that too many people outside still think of this place as a lunatic asylum!' There was a terrible pause. The unspeakable had been spoken. That was what we were: barmy. That was where we were: in the bin.

It is true that today this is thought less strongly by the people *outside* than the people *inside*. The old stone-carved legend, IVYBRIDGE ASYLUM, has been covered up by a brightly painted board, MOORHAVEN PSYCHIATRIC HOSPITAL. But everyone knew what was underneath the board. The awful fact that here he is, in a lunatic asylum, is almost enough in itself to drive the newcomer out of what wits he has left. *Didn't think I was a nutcase.*

Newcomers naturally react differently according to their different backgrounds. I think I settled down more quickly than any other of my near-contemporaries, except one: and we both had a preliminary advantage. One of us had been to a public school, and one of us to prison. Evelyn Waugh, in *Decline and Fall*, wrote that 'anyone who has been to an English public school will always feel comparatively at home in prison.' It is a serious point. Lord Pethick Lawrence, writing of the time when he was imprisoned for his support of the suffragettes, said that at prison exercise he felt exactly as he had done at his preparatory school. The similarity of boarding schools, prisons, mental hospitals, and perhaps the services as they once were, is more than a matter of living a regulated and institutional life. They are all societies governed by a *we – they* relationship: societies with a great gulf fixed in their midst. Masters and pupils, officers and other ranks, prison staff and prisoners, hospital staff and patients: they are set apart on either side.

Nowhere is the gulf wider, I conjecture, nor the crossing more difficult, than in a mental hospital. Even at Moorhaven few of the staff knew how wide it was. Here is an example. One day a young man announced his intention of breaking out, along with one of the girl patients, and going into Plymouth on the booze. This was not a very hard thing to do, as they were both in open wards, and the buses were only a few hundred yards away. He had done this kind of thing several times before, and always with disastrous consequences. Everyone in the ward, and most people in the neighbouring wards, knew of his intention, for he spent most of the day borrowing money for his spree. He was a well-liked lad, though clearly mentally sick (the upper half of his body was covered with self-inflicted cigarette burns). A further smash would have even more disastrous consequences.

A single word to a nurse by one patient during the day would have been enough to put a stop to it. The word was not spoken. It was not spoken because it would have been *sneaking*. The sneak at school, the trusty in prison, is shunned by his fellows; and so it is in a mental hospital. If you leave the tight group of *us*, and have any dealings with *them*, you are in No Man's Land. The only security a patient has is in the company of his fellow-sufferers. He dare not risk that security by any dealings with the enemy.

This young man was brought back by the police, early in the morning. He went back to the closed wards, broke out again and went to prison for a long time. I have a note in my diary of my last sight of him. I called him Fred.

> Fred has been moved to the 'big house' for greater security after his escapade. He was escorted out of the ward, fairly quietly, by six of the largest and toughest male nurses, assembled from all over the hospital. His bearing was proud as he went, slowly stubbing out a cigarette on the back of his hand. There was a panic half an hour earlier, when he disappeared, and was found lurking in the wash-room with a kitchen knife. But he came out and returned the knife when asked politely, and in any case the kitchen knives here can hardly cut a fried egg, which no doubt is just as well.
>
> Shortly before Fred left Jack came out of his little semi-private ward to see him, ever anxious to take part in any war against authority, and temporarily forgetting his new slogan, BE A FREND TO ALL MAN. Despite his great strength Jack is very wobbly on his feet, owing to the drugs and his long spell in bed. He lurched towards Fred and shook him by the hand. 'Fred o' man,' he said 'Fred o' man.' Fred snorted. 'Come on,' coaxed Jack. 'You'n me's going down Plymouth together today and we won't half sort those copper bastards out.' Jack then fell flat on his back and was carried back to bed.

'Only connect,' said E. M. Forster, and it is a phrase much used by psychiatrists, indeed nowadays by political writers and practically everybody else. It has almost become a cant phrase. But no doubt failure of connection – with other people, or between the different parts of one's own personality – is one way of describing most mental illnesses. A doctor cannot do his patient much good, barring the more severe and uncertain physical treatments (heavy drugs, electric shocks, lobotomy), unless a connection between minds is established.

To come back to little Bill in the bed opposite: the moment when a patient is most vulnerable, most anxious for companionship, most ready to make an effort to communicate with a doctor, is immediately after he comes into hospital. The practice at Moorhaven was that the patient saw no doctor, apart from the hurried duty doctor, for several days. He was kept 'under observation', with the nurses reporting regularly on his behaviour. It is true that the doctor, especially if he has no previous knowledge of the patient, is better equipped for his task when he has some observed information to guide him. It was also said that the pause gave the patient time to settle down. This was so, though not quite in the sense the authorities meant it. For by the time he came to see his doctor the patient had clutched at the one bastion in his crumbled world: the security of the ward. He had emphatically become 'one of us', and not 'one of them'. He had heard a great many stories, most of them untrue, about the casual cruelties of nurses, and the much more profound, soul-destroying cruelties of doctors.

It is in these first few hours that the doctor has by far his best chance of establishing an honest relationship with his patient. That is the time when he might be able to prevent the gulf opening. Once it has opened his task is much more difficult. The patient, after a few days, has grown accustomed to the thought that he is a nutcase, that he is in the bin. He will accept, for convenience of relations with the staff, the theory that he is in an ordinary hospital, but in his heart he does not believe it for a moment, and nor do his mates.

However, though I think this policy of lengthy preliminary observation is a gravely mistaken one, I must add that it is not within the power of most hospitals to change it, even should they so wish. The doctors were, and are, heavily overworked. On a careful, rational calculation of what was needed for the proper treatment of the patients in their charge, seven junior doctors at Moorhaven were trying to do the work of thirteen. Senior consultants would have had to work roughly twice the number of hours each week implied in their contracts. Some of them did. Some of them, since then, have probably become patients themselves. I was fortunate in my own doctor. At the time I did not think he was paying me nearly enough attention. I now realize he was paying me a good deal more than the average patient (I suppose an articulate patient made a change, and may even have been a help to him). Yet though I had this favoured treatment I did not see him often enough, and above all I did not see him soon enough. This was not his fault.[1] I record it without rancour. There was nothing rancorous to remember of Moorhaven, except some of the food, but fortunately since I grew up I have never bothered too much about food, though enjoying good stuff when it is about.

When I left Moorhaven I wondered if I was 'cured': not a very sensible question. It was two years more before I could give up the barbiturates, and giving them up was not much fun. 'Cured?' The dear Lord knows. But it was an interesting experience. I did not enjoy it, I have no desire to repeat it, but I cannot be altogether sorry it happened. I know a little more about one set of devils. And I made friends, among both staff and patients, whom I otherwise might not have met. And I smile to myself whenever anyone passes me the bread.

1. See *Medical Staffing in Psychiatric Hospitals*, by Robert A. Blair, Kenneth F. Weeks and Charles P. Hellon. *The British Journal of Psychiatry*, 1964.

14 Bristol

Had I died instead of going to Moorhaven, my life might have been said to have had an accountable pattern. Gibson, they would have said (charming chap in some ways) was unable to come to terms with the world. His Dissenting upbringing clashed too much with his passions, including his fleshly passions. Since he could not rid himself of the first, and could not restrain the second, the tension was bound to be intolerable. Best out of it, poor fellow.

Artistically, no doubt, the last ten years of my life have been an anticlimax. I was in every sense a miserable creature for several years after Moorhaven. From this situation I was rescued, gradually and painfully, by my second marriage in 1966. Rosemary had worked for the BBC, partly in the Features Department, and had some experience of temperamental broadcasters. The circumstances in which I met and proposed to her were romantically bizarre. I forbear from setting them down, partly because they would not be believed.

Even our marriage, when achieved, did not have an altogether propitious beginning. We were married in the Congregational Church at Croydon, by my old friend Noel Calvin. (Noel was the only Congregational minister ever to be President of a branch of the Society for the Preservation of Beers from the Wood, an office in which I succeeded him after his sadly early death.) The day before, I had travelled to London. Rosemary had packed a case and we left it at Waterloo station, in the luggage office – a precaution against waggish friends. We then had a drink and I bade her a warm farewell before she caught her train to Croydon. As I was doing so, my trousers fell down (it was a new suit which did not fit). This caused something of a stir among the commuters. However, the trousers remained up during the ceremony next day, which passed off well enough, though it started a little late, as Noel and I and John Mason (my best man) had found a good pub up the road. Taxi to Waterloo, and off to Bournemouth (it was a working honeymoon, following the Australian rugby team on tour). Half way to Bournemouth we realized we had left Rosemary's case at Waterloo. She had a handbag and what she stood up in. It was just before Christmas, and it was days before we could get the case sent on. To have one dress to wear on your honeymoon does not put a bride into the best of tempers. We had been in the hotel about ten minutes when the telephone went. I moved to take the call, caught my foot on the carpet, fell awkwardly, and broke my ankle. Rosemary spent the first morning of her marriage in Poole General Hospital while they put the plaster on. We had with us, as appropriate reading, *Busman's Honeymoon*, by Dorothy L. Sayer's and one of the characters says 'There be more to marriage than four bare legs in a bed.' 'He can say that again,' said Rosemary, surveying my swathed limb.

In 1964 I had moved to Bristol. There was not enough for me to do at Plymouth any more, and I did not want to go to London. I wanted to keep my freedom, the precious though precarious liberty of the freelance, and Bristol seemed the proper compromise. The BBC, and particularly Desmond Hawkins, had gone out of their way to be helpful to me during and after my time in hospital, but I was not broadcasting very well, and my own problems apart it was a difficult time for regional broadcasting. It became increasingly obvious that the days of our beloved West of England Home Service were numbered.

I am not qualified to discuss the politics of the modern BBC, but the outline of what happened is fairly clear. The BBC's character was permanently changed when, after the introduction of commercial television, the decision was taken to compete for viewers in *quantity*. This altered the character of the Corporation, and soon had repercussions in sound radio. Many men in sound radio, faced with their shrinking audience figures, felt that the product had to be transformed to survive. The new recipe was to be pop music and (on the strength of that inept American analogy), local radio.

The establishment of a chain of local radio stations, however small their budgets, would cost money. With television preoccupied at vast expense with its battle with the commercial tycoons, there was no chance of getting any more from the licence fees. Any further expenditure on sound radio would mean that money must be taken away from sound radio services already existing. The natural candidates for sacrifice were the English Regions and the Third Programme, and so it proved, after years of argument and a good deal of double-talk.

There was a special irony to this, so far as we in the west were concerned, in that some of the men who had done most to build up the region's broadcasting now found themselves responsible for dismantling it. When Frank Gillard retired from his post as Director of Sound Broadcasting he came to Bristol for a farewell party. I was asked to this party. I took the invitation as a compliment, since it was otherwise confined to members of staff. I suppose my long association with West Region and with Frank were held to qualify me. I arrived a little late. The staff lined the walls. Frank, in the middle of the room, was talking to two venerable ladies who I think were charwomen (perhaps the only people present whose jobs were not threatened). The atmosphere was a long way from convivial. I hastened to relieve the charwomen, and the following conversation took place:

F.G.; Hallo, Alan, I didn't expect to see you here.
A.G.; Well, I suppose they needed an independent witness for the demo.

I joined the hushed ranks round the walls. After a little Desmond Hawkins (by now Controller, West Region, the last man to hold the post) briefly proposed Frank's health. The only sentence I remember is: 'When I heard that Frank was retiring, I thought that whatever happens I am going to get my resignation in first' (as he had done). Frank, unruffled, addressed the gathering. He drew a graphic picture of the great days of broadcasting in the west, the days of expansion; he dwelt upon the team spirit that had developed under his leadership. He recalled famous and familiar names and programmes. He made little jokes, struck old chords. In no time at all he had his audience with him. Here and there a tear crept down a cheek. Afterwards we clustered round him, happily, full of sweetness and light. Nothing, of course, had changed. I mention this incident not only to illustrate Frank Gillard's compelling charm but the depth of feeling which still existed about the West Region among those who worked in it, even though their fruits lay withered and strewn about them.

There were many casualties in the destruction of the Region. Some had to take jobs in other departments or in local radio, jobs which did not (at least in the first place) appeal to them. Some found themselves with no jobs at all, though of course there were safeguards for established staff. Some, as a result of negotiations by the Association of Broadcasting Staff, kept jobs which were hardly real jobs, struggling to find things with which to fill their time, increasingly and inevitably content to be office boys for London, where all the decisions were now taken.

This was one of the times when I was pleased to be a freelance. I had at least more room for manœuvre than many old friends and colleagues. It was, of course, alarming that my principal source of income should vanish, and it happened at the worst possible time, just as I had embarked on a new marriage and a new family. However, I had managed to make sufficient reputation as a broadcaster to get a fair amount of work on the network; and because I had not been tied to the BBC I had one or two other interests which I could develop. There was one very bad year when the income tax people had to be shown every figure before they would accept that my profits were so small. But we survived. One reason for this was that the BBC's Natural History unit continued to be based in Bristol. Another was that, thanks to the sports editors of *The Times*, the *Sunday Times*, the *Sunday Telegraph* and *The Guardian*, I began to do more cricket and rugby reporting for the press. So, as I write, we are still living in Bristol, and happy to be, and making ends nearly meet, which is as much as I have ever been able to do.

Of the two principal cities of the west I had always preferred Plymouth to Bristol, and the first years in Bristol did nothing to change my view (though wherever I lived at that time I would have been in no mood to like it). But I have grown fond of the city, and shall not complain if I end my days in or near it.

By an accident of neighbourhood, I came to know another great man in Bristol, Professor Charles MacInnes. He was long retired when I first knew him, in his mid-seventies, but fuller of beans than any man of that age that I have met. Charles MacInnes had lost his sight, through measles, at the age of eight. He learned Braille, he learned to type, he went to Dalhousie University in Canada – he was a tough Canadian Scot, a Buchan type, and he liked to quote:

From the lone shieling of the misty island
Mountains divide us, and the waste of seas –
Yet still the blood is strong, the heart is Highland,
And we in dreams behold the Hebrides.

This he would pronounce with a pungent Canadian accent, breaking off from time to time, as he always did when he spoke poetry, to say, 'Bygord that's a good line, a bloody good line.' We had the same primitive reactions to poetry.

He was never to behold the Hebrides, but he came to Britain, to Balliol, where he turned cartwheels in the quadrangle and rowed in eights (not the first eight, to be sure, but one of those more cheerful boats near the bottom of the river). He was a scholar and a writer, and in 1919 became a lecturer in history at Bristol. He became Professor of Imperial History, a title which he retained, Emeritus, after his retirement. He continued to work a full day, right up to his death, when he was nearly eighty. Indeed, he used to walk down from Clifton to his chambers in the town, by himself, until one day they moved a lamp-post without warning him. After that he worked mostly at home, but he was always out and about at some committee, or lecture, or party. He did not want to die at all. He felt fit, and had all his faculties except for the one which he had long before ceased to count. He was in no way a figure of pathos. I have been told that in his days at the University of Bristol he had the reputation of being an awkward customer, and I can believe it. Epstein got him right. It was a strange feeling to sit in Charles MacInnes's room, with the Professor sitting on the sofa, and the Epstein bust looking over his shoulder. Epstein could not capture, in bronze, the ruddy cheeks or the mop of white hair, but he had the lift of the chin, the sense of challenge, almost of arrogance, of a man who simultaneously welcomed life and defied it. MacInnes's acquaintance was vast and his comments upon those he had met were free. I would read to him sometimes. We read *Zuleika Dobson*, which oddly enough he had missed; and *Slide Rule*, Nevil Shute's autobiography; and the Compton Mackenzie novels about Ben Nevis (the man, not the mountain). These readings would be interspersed by the Professor's reminiscences of Beerbohm, or Norway (Shute's real name), or Old Compo. We also read much poetry. He was suspicious of anything later than Robert Bridges, but I managed to earn a few reluctant marks for Charles Causley.

Bristol is a good place for rugby and cricket. The rugby side, in most seasons one of the best in the country, has a long reputation for open, attacking play. The cricket ground, which I have come to know better than any other cricket ground, is a curious, ramshackle affair, but not without character. The first thing that takes the eye is the clock tower on the pavilion, because it is not in the middle of the roof but about two-thirds of the way along, creating a cock-eyed effect which is not altogether inappropriate to Gloucestershire cricket. The pavilion has recently undergone some internal surgery, but was put together bit by bit over a long period, in many different shapes and styles: a press-box, a bar or a balcony added on, whenever it occurred to somebody. Before the renovations it was a difficult place in which to find your way around, and more than one broadcaster has missed his cue by taking a wrong staircase (I would not say it is easy territory even now). I wrote of it a few years ago thus:

> If you want to go to the room next door, you are likely to have to find a flight of stairs, which takes you down and round to the back, and then find another flight of stairs. The door you think you want will be jammed. You try another: it opens, but it is the wrong one. Suddenly you are lost.

> You catch a glimpse of the cricket, unattainably distant, through a high attic window. You grow desperate, try any door you can see, burst in on aged members and wake them up, flush a committee or two, and thankfully emerge where you started. At least, you usually do. There may be a few heroes still trudging round.

If you knew that old pavilion you would find the exaggeration pardonable.

The West of England Home Service duly departed, and, so far as Bristol is concerned, Radio Bristol has taken its place. Local radio is not much help to battered freelances such as I, not from lack of goodwill but lack of cash. Apart from personal considerations I doubt if it is an improvement on the old pattern of broadcasting. Travelling as I do round the country I hear some dreadful things on local radio. Nevertheless I must put in a word for Radio Bristol. David Waine and Bill Salisbury (both former regional producers) have maintained a high standard of literacy and dignity in their programmes, while taking due account of local interests and local pressures. It shows it can be done. After all, you do not need to tune to local radio nowadays to hear that someone has literally flown down the wing, or that there is a crash bid for a new probe, or that the government is showing a lack of ertia: or for the constant, hopeless misuse of words such as (to take two) 'sensation' and 'phenomenon'. Radio Bristol suffers from these faults less than many network programmes. A few years ago there was a sensational and phenomenal murder in Blackpool, and it was reported by the BBC's man-on-the-spot 'in such exuberant terms that you would have thought Blackpool had won the Cup'. It was David Waine who made that criticism, and made sure that the joyous overtones were removed before the piece was allowed to go out on his own station. There is still taste, and restraint, and decency around in the BBC, and not least in Bristol. Perhaps the West of England Home Service did not die for nothing.

15 Beulah

It would make a more ringing title for my last chapter – less a chapter than an afterword – if I could call it 'Great Deliverance', as Billy Bray called his chapel, or even 'Hallelujah', as the Bible Christians were wont to call their children. Yet I end, as I began, within the ambience of *chapel*. Tyndale Baptist Church, Clifton, counts me among one of its more erratic attenders, but Rosemary (who is only a Dissenter by marriage) has become deeply attached to its fellowship, runs the playgroup, looks after the creche when it is her turn; and my small children trot along with her on Sunday mornings, experiencing many of the same emotions, and even singing some of the same hymns, as I did at their age. They seem to enjoy it, perhaps because they know they do not have to go if they do not wish to.

One of the hymns they are not nowadays taught to sing is 'Beulah Land'. 'Beulah' is a name sanctified by the Bible, and by Bunyan, and has the additional advantage that nobody quite knows what it means. There have been chapels called Beulah, and there was a Sankey chorus, which Isaac Foot liked to quote,

> O Beulah land, sweet Beulah land,
> As on thy highest mount I stand,
> I look away across the sea,
> Where mansions are prepared for me,
> And view the shining glory shore;
> My heaven, my home, for evermore!

It went with a good swing to a tune that was a mixture of

'Sweet Genevieve' and 'The Red Flag'. According to Bunyan the pilgrims still had difficulties ahead when they reached the land of Beulah, but they were through the Valley of the Shadow of Death, and out of the reach of Giant Despair, and within sight of the City. I think – well, sometimes I think – that I have got as far as Beulah.

I am glad that I was brought up a Dissenter. I believe the good qualities of such an upbringing at least balance the bad. I am glad I was not brought up a Roman Catholic, or a communist, or a Jehovah's Witness, or a stockbroker. In 1972 Kenneth Young published a book called *Chapel* (Eyre Methuen) and sub-titled it with a reference to 'the joyous days and prayerful nights' of the Nonconformists. I am glad of those joyous days and prayerful nights. How good it is that Dissenters can still laugh at themselves, without forsaking their fathers! Mr Young tells a story about a local preacher. It was a new story to me, and yet I swear I have heard that (Cornish?) local preacher.

> 'Now boys and girls I 'ave a special word for you this morning, a very good word and one I want you to remember. It is a five letter word and I will spell it out for you. Haitch, Haye, Bee, Hi, Tee: '*Abit.*'

The Band of Hope songs. I used to sing this with my father:

> Merry Dick you soon would know,
> If you lived in Jackson's Row,
> Each day with a smiling face
> Dick is ready in his place.
> Should you ever with him meet
> In the shop or in the street,
> You will find him blithe and gay,
> Singing out this merry lay,

MY drink is water bright, water bright, water bright,
MY drink is water bright, from the crystal stream!

And, more dolefully, this:

Father, dear father, come home with me now,
The clock in the steeple's struck one;
You promised dear mother that you would come home
As soon as your day's work was done;
The fire has gone out, and the house is all dark,
And mother's been waiting since tea;
With poor brother Benny asleep in her arms,
And no one to help her but me.
Come home, come ho-o-ome, etc.

Father and I did not sing these songs entirely seriously, you understand. They were period pieces even in my childhood. But they had a long life. Many years later, in the vestry of Kingsbridge Baptist Chapel, I came across a leaflet of 'Temperance Choruses set to Popular Tunes', which I purloined, and still possess. This is my favourite (the tune is 'Come, Follow': it is intended to be sung as a round, and guaranteed to make any party go):

No, wine won't hurt you, hurt you, hurt you, not a little bit,
If you never swallow, swallow, swallow, if you never swallow, swallow it!
So refuse it, so refuse it, so refuse it and keep fit!

The author is Christine I. Tinling, among whose other works, we are informed, is 'Sidelights from Shakespeare on the Alcohol Problem'. This, alas! I have never been able to trace, but would readily give a bottle of Scotch to anyone who could.

In *Sankey's Songs and Solos*, the old editions, there is a hymn

– not a temperance hymn, but coming from the same tradition – which tells us of the death-bed of Little Willie.

'I would like to die,' said Willie, 'if my papa could die too,
But he says he isn't ready, 'cos he's got too much to do;
And my little sister Nellie says that I must surely die,
And that she and mama – then she stopped because it made her cry.

'There will be none but the holy – I shall know no more of sin;
There I'll see Mama and Nellie, for I know he'll let them in;
But I'll have to tell the angel, when I meet him at the door,
That he must excuse my papa, 'cos he couldn't leave the store.'

Another Sankey hymn:

Mariners we,
Sailing life's sea

shortly followed by

Boats for the Kingdom
Set sail every hour.

A church notice:

MOUNT PLEASANT FREE CHURCH

Morning 10.45: Subject – 'A Peep Into Hell'
The choir will sing the anthem: 'O Taste and See'

The extempore prayers: I have told you that we never

believed in praying from a book, because the Holy Spirit would put words in our mouths. An old lady declaring, 'Lord, I am climbing Zion's hill,' and the class leader chiming in, 'Stick your toes in, Jane wench.' A husband, still himself uncertain, but married to a Salvationist, praying, 'Lord, make me as good a man as my old woman' – and a prayer meeting near Doncaster, where someone who had already said his prayer was listening to his friend's effort, and was moved to add, 'Aye, do Lord, I forgot to axe thi that'; and the worshipper who, running short of material, paused and said, 'Now Lord I will tell thee an anecdote . . .'

Yes, it was all very funny: but there is no need quite to laugh your head off. The hymns included some magnificent pieces of religious poetry, as well as the doggerel. Even the doggerel did not always miss its mark. 'Father, dear father, come home with me now': I dare say my own father had had to fetch my grandfather from the pub a few times late on pay night. Even Little Willie, whose father had to be excused, ' 'cos he couldn't leave the store': he had a point. And the extempore prayers, if they were sometimes bogus, and sometimes routine as any liturgy, did involve a kind of genial familiarity with the Almighty. Where else do you find that in the Christian tradition? You find it in the New Testament. It was with such a friendly mixture of casualness and solemnity that Jesus approached God. He might well have added, as a footnote to a prayer by one of his disciples, *Aye, Lord, do; I forgot to axe thi that.*

As for the sense of guilt: it is true that many Nonconformists have wallowed in guilt, the better to enjoy their salvation. When I was a small boy I used to run to the coal cellar and dirty my knees before Friday evening's bath. It seemed a waste of a good bath unless you had plenty to wash off, and it was splendid to look on the horrible black water, once you were out of it and clean. No doubt guilt complexes have accounted for many mental illnesses. But not all defects of character can be ascribed to mental illness, or vice versa. I think on the whole Charles Wesley – 'that blessed sense of guilt' – was right. Who would really wish to be an amoral creature? If we cannot be guiltless, the next best thing is to be guilty. My father would now say, 'Ah, but it is better than either to be redeemed.' I cannot altogether agree with father, but I have no doubt it is better to be wrong with Jesus Christ than to be right without him.

The great perception of Jesus was that God was a loving father. He made this assertion in the face of terrible evidence to the contrary. All the great edifices of theology are no more than an attempt to reconcile the observable plight of mankind with the belief that 'feyther do truly love 'ee'. It is in this perception that Jesus is, for me, a revelation of God: and if his belief was wrong then I find no sense, no comfort, in either God or man.

But I notice that I am being overcome by the old Dissenting custom of preaching on every possible occasion. Finally, then, brethren, some good things that shine through the pain: the line of the moor at Ilkley, the comforting Leyton trams at night, St Ives Bay, the feel of a rugby scrum working well (when Totnes were beating Buckfastleigh for the first time in twenty years); taking five wickets in five balls in a house match (it was a freak, but it is my only athletic boast, and the batsmen who can confirm it are still, I trust, alive); lunch on a spring day at *The Bear of Rodborough*; the expression on the face of the first girl I ever kissed – it was a mixture of surprise and cunning – under a harvest moon; the Totnes United Free Church choir, and how the basses came rolling in with

The lions do LACK and suffer HUNG-er

– *but they that seek the Lord*, it goes on with many complicated repetitions, *shall want no manner of thing that is good*. And my children: more than anything else in my life, I have had pleasure from my children. I have not written much about them, because they will have plenty to say for themselves in due course. Anthony and Andrew, my sons by my first marriage, are safely through Oxford. Adam is seven, Felicity three. Life cannot have been too bad if you have a daughter in middle age and feel able to call her Felicity.

And now (dare I borrow Robertson-Glasgow's closing sentence? I will risk it): and now, tomorrow.